Advanced Praise for *Journaling for the Soul*

If you think *journaling* is just sitting down and writing out dense pages of prose in a notebook, read on! Yes, there is a notebook involved, but Deborah Haddix offers a resplendent banquet of ways to use this practice to communicate with God. *Journaling for the Soul* offers a personalized meal for everyone, or maybe many meals for everyone. When I finished reading her book, I wanted to grab my notebook and try out several of the offerings I had never heard of before: CliffsNotes; Daily Dot Points; and the quirkily-named Squish-It Prayer Journaling.

Sybil MacBeth
Author, *Praying in Color: Drawing a New Path to God*

Whether you are a seasoned journal keeper or just getting started, this book provides a marvelous roadmap to help your journaling practice flourish. Deborah Haddix brings years of journaling experience to this comprehensive guide. Her pages are filled with a myriad of ways to grow your faith and connect more deeply with God, all while applying and enjoying the proven, positive benefits of journal writing. Dive in and embrace Deborah's work; you'll be glad you did!

Kathy Bornarth, MA, LPC
President, National Association of Christian Journal Writers www.nacjw.com
Author, *Stories of Transformation Through Journal Writing* and
The Friendship Guidebook: A Journaling Roadmap to Making Friends

If you have ever wondered what all the excitement is about journaling, here is your answer! *Journaling for the Soul* is an absolute treasure of not only *"Why"* but *"How To"* journal! Packed full of ideas for artists and list-makers, in-depth Bible students and the beginners. Warning: you will likely develop an addiction to journaling once you try some of these techniques!

Lisa W. Smith, Bible study leader
Author of *Oscar the Extraordinary Hummingbird* and *The Wisdom Tree*

Deborah Haddix jump starts the journals we've considered writing for years with her handbook, *Journaling for the Soul: Slow Down, Replenish, Exhale.* She offers a collection of methods, which are user-friendly, flexible, non-intimidating and Scripturally-based. Like me, her readers will discover journal types that suit their personalities or seasons of life and draw into a deeper relationship with Christ, drenching their thirsty souls through the timeless art of writing.

Sherry Schumann
Prayer Co-Director, Christian Grandparenting Network
Author, *The Christmas Bracelet*

Who knew the pathway to going deeper could be so fun? *Journaling for the Soul* is a valuable resource for the spiritually hungry. In this handbook, Deborah begins with a beautifully written introduction to the reader showing the ways journaling can help us lean into God's loving presence and tend to our souls. Next, she offers a treasure trove of ideas for journaling. There is something for everyone. This book makes it all accessible by breaking each method down and then listing materials, steps and suggestions.

Susan Borgstrom, MA, BCCC
Director, Awakening in Nature & Certified Christian Life Coach

Having been a Biblical "journaler" for almost two decades, I am thrilled that Deborah has written a book to help my fellow believers in Jesus get started on recording their own daily time with the LORD. I started writing my requests to Him during a very difficult time in my life, but little did I know that my loving Papa was getting me trained for even harder times ahead. Through family turmoil, difficult days in my husband's fight with terminal cancer, and the general chaos of life, not to mention the tough counseling issues we as counselors encounter, journaling took me from "requests" to "pleas" to "angry whys" and on to "grateful singing." Now I know why there are so many psalms of complaint in Scripture, not just from a trained Biblical point of view, but also from the emotional realm of personal experience. We are all "little psalmists" writing our praises and laments for the next generation (or two) to draw them closer to the LORD. Journal on!

Kathi Brown, BCBC
Director of Counseling Ministries
River Valley Church
Grants Pass, OR

Journaling for the Soul:

SLOW DOWN, REPLENISH, EXHALE

— A Handbook of Journaling Methods —

By Deborah Haddix

Warner Press, Inc
Warner Press and "WP" logo are trademarks of Warner Press, Inc

Journaling for the Soul: Slow Down, Replenish, Exhale
A Handbook of Journaling Methods
Written by Deborah Haddix
Copyright ©2018 Deborah Haddix
Cover and layout copyright ©2018 Warner Press, Inc

ISBN: 978-1-68434-100-9
E-book ISBN: 978-1-68434-101-6
Printed in the USA

Cover Design: Curtis Corzine
Layout: Katie Miller
Editors: Karen Rhodes, Tammy Tilley

All rights reserved.

Requests for information should be sent to:
Warner Press Inc
2902 Enterprise Dr
P.O. Box 2499
Anderson, IN 46013
www.warnerpress.org

For my dad,
Donald Leemon Jones.
You left fingerprints of love and grace all over our lives.

"*Journaling*
is one of the most
overlooked and undervalued

spiritual disciplines

· · · ·

It is the way we document
what God is doing in our lives."

Mark Batterson

Contents

A Collection of Methods

Prayer Journaling

Scripture Journaling

Soul Friendship Journaling

Soul Searching Journaling

Journaling Challenges

Bibliography

With Deepest Gratitude to:

The generous bloggers and authors who granted permission for their journaling methods to be included in this handbook: Mindy Caliguire, Betsy de Cruz, Sybil MacBeth, Barb Raveling, Kim Young.

The enthusiastic and dedicated journaling methods proofing team who gave of their time and talent to proofread sheet after sheet of methods: Amy Ballard, Susan Borgstrom, Melissa Flanagan, Nancy Grunkemeyer, Kara Haddix, Claire Huggins, Lori Kirl, Katie Rich, Julie Takseraas, Glenda Taylor, Karen Wooldridge, Kim Young.

The incredible members of the book launch team: Kathy Bornarth, Kathi Brown, Linda Cabiness, Vicki Gabbard, Don Haddix, Melissa Mortensen, Monica Rice, Sherry Schumann, Lisa Smith, Karen Stringer, Glenda Taylor, Roberta Vinyard, Melissa Waters, Kim Young.

Two behind-the-scenes ladies who donated hours of their time in loving support of this project: Claire Huggins, Glenda Taylor.

Welcome

to the wonderful world of *Journaling for the Soul!*

I feel so incredibly blessed to be able to share my passion for journaling for the soul with you through this handbook. Intentional soul care is essential to our well-being. Personally, I have found journaling to be one of the most effective and meaningful ways to fulfill my soul's need.

An invaluable tool for soul care, journaling calls me to *attend*, permits me to *enjoy*, and *draws me to God*. Versatile across the spiritual disciplines, the many journaling methods offer me choice, flexibility, and deeper communion with my heavenly Father. Praying in Color, Verse Mapping, or Counting Gifts—it doesn't matter—whichever method I choose to engage in, I am drawn into conversation with God, and my gaze is turned upon Him.

I'm aware that it might sound like I'm a dyed-in-the-wool, always-been-journaling type of girl, but that hasn't always been my story. In all honesty, I've only been journaling for the benefit of my soul for a couple of years.

My Story

Writing has almost always been a painful task. I owned one of those little lock-and-key diaries when I was a girl. It was cute, but I didn't write in it.

As a language arts teacher, I observed journaling time with my students because it was good for them, but I rarely journaled myself. I'm not sure which was more painful, staring at a blank page that needed to be filled, or actually having to perform the act of writing.

Formulating thoughts, getting them into words (enough to fill a page), and putting pen to paper simply required more energy than I wanted to expend. I wasn't wired that way. The value could not possibly be worth it!

In more recent years, friends have from time to time shared with me just how much they treasure journaling. They have shared its benefits for spiritual growth and deep communion with God. As valued friends in a deep and growing relationship with my heavenly Father, I wanted what they had. I listened, and on occasion I gave it another try as I hoped to find what they found. Still…nothing.

Until one summer morning a couple of years ago.

Thank God for His grace and for never giving up on me! Out of His lavish love for me and through several God-orchestrated appointments—workshop presentations, books, Sunday sermons—God revealed to me that there was another way!

All those years, my definition of journaling had been oh, so narrow. In my mind, journaling was a task: "seated in a quiet spot, pen in hand, blank page before you—too much effort to formulate thoughts into words, and too much work to write out the words."

What freedom to be set loose that summer as God showed me I had been uniquely wired with gifts, talents, and interests that I could use not only for my own enjoyment, but also for connecting with Him! Journaling can be fun and can look any way I want it to look, and it can involve things I enjoy: paper crafting, color, photography, and Scripture.

When it comes right down to it, journaling just to be journaling is pretty much useless. But journaling for the purpose of connecting with God? Now that gives the process meaning that goes far beyond the act of processing thoughts or writing them down. Journaling for my soul, in whatever shape it takes, draws me to God and brings me into daily conversation with Him.

I am excited to share some of my discoveries about journaling for the soul with you in this handbook. I hope this book will inspire you to tap into your own unique God-wiring and encourage you to uncover ways that feed your soul and bring you closer to God.

This collection of journaling for the soul methods spans the spectrum of spiritual disciplines. Among them are several that speak directly to my heart, draw me in, and create channels for me to spend time cultivating a practice that I am convinced encourages and enables my spiritual growth and nourishes my soul.

I pray you will find the same. May you be blessed, as I have been, to discover journaling methods that not only encourage and enable your spiritual growth but also provide needed nourishment for your soul.

SLOW DOWN, REPLENISH, EXHALE

What is Journaling for the Soul?

- Simply defined, journaling for the soul is a way to connect with God at a deeper level.

- Foundational to this discipline is the journaling process—one that invites us to record our experiences, observations, ideas, reflections, and such on a regular basis.

- Journaling is a tool for soul care. Used as a spiritual discipline, it helps us grow in grace, experience truth, and discover His character.

- The process of journaling for the soul strengthens other spiritual disciplines.

- Journaling our Bible study can lead us to new insights. Combine journaling with prayer, and our prayers become more concrete, which in turn facilitates better communication with our heavenly Father. Incorporated into the discipline of simplicity, journaling leads to genuine and unhindered praise and worship.

- Journaling for the soul is about *engaging*...

  › Our mind and our body as we become focused and involved.

  › Our creativity as we consider our God-wiring and discover fun and meaningful ways to meet with Him.

  › With other spiritual disciplines. For example, journaling will help you engage with the Bible text, moving you from the act of reading for information to reading for transformation.

Journaling for the soul helps us move away from our old mindset that spiritual practices are draining obligations and helps us view them as practices that connect us to God, His grace, His energy, and His joy. It's a tool for engaging more intentionally and consistently with God, a means for getting to know His heart (see John 17:3).

May you discover methods of journaling for the soul that speak directly to your heart, draw you in, and create channels that enable you to cultivate a practice that engages you more intentionally and consistently with your heavenly Father, helping you to know Him. And may your soul be nourished as it is filled with God's grace, His energy, and His joy.

Why is Journaling for the Soul Important?

Journaling for the soul is an important spiritual discipline.

First, journaling is biblical. From the beginning, our spiritual history has rested on God's written word. God spoke, and man wrote. I have not actually taken the time to count it myself, but I have heard that the words "Write this," "Write down," or "Write" can be found approximately 166 times in the Bible.

Look closely at these verses. When you do, not only will you find the command to write, you will discover the WHY.

Revelation 21:5—*He who was seated on the throne said, "I am making everything new!" Then he said, "Write this down, for these words are trustworthy and true."*

Exodus 17:14—*Then the LORD said to Moses, "Write this on a scroll as something to be remembered and make sure that Joshua hears it."*

Habakkuk 2:2—*Then the LORD replied: "Write down the revelation and make it plain on tablets so that a herald may run with it."*

Exodus 34:27—*The LORD said to Moses, "Write down these words, for in accordance with these words I have made a covenant with you and with Israel."*

Deuteronomy 31:19—*Now write down this song and teach it to the Israelites and have them sing it.*

- Writing solidifies God's words in your soul (Revelation 21:5).

- It makes the words of God more likely to be remembered (Exodus 17:4).

- Putting pen to paper or chalk to canvas makes God's words easier to share (Habakkuk 2:2).

- Writing indicates a commitment to action or follow through (Exodus 34:27).

- It puts information in a form for teaching and self-study (Deuteronomy 31:19).

Secondly, journaling for the soul meets some of our soul's deep needs while providing us with other valuable life benefits. By God's design, the soul was created with many needs, two of which are:

- The need to be with God (Psalm 63:1, 143:6).

- The need for rest (Psalm 116:7; Jeremiah 6:16; Matthew 11:29).

Journaling for the soul helps us be with God:

- The spiritual discipline of journaling creates space, focuses our attention, and builds relationship. We live in a noisy, crowded world.

- Journaling invites us into quiet. It forces us to be still and creates needed space for meeting with God.

- Involving the mind and the body, journaling helps us stay present. It clears the clutter of our much-too-easily distracted minds, helping us focus on communing with God.

- As we connect with God, we are drawn closer to Him. In this position, we are able to look more closely at what is happening in our hearts and minds. Here we can see more clearly the work the Holy Spirit is doing and listen more intently as God speaks wisdom in our lives.

Capturing this work—what we see, what we hear, our thoughts, our questions, our responses—helps us grow in deeper relationship with God. It clarifies our understanding of the nature of God, provides a way for us to reflect upon and remember His character, and helps us build an intimate, authentic relationship with Him. It brings us to a fuller knowledge of God.

Our soul also needs rest. Jesus knew the power of a rested soul. In fact, it is recorded for us that He regularly went off to a solitary place. Jesus, the Son of God, pulled away from His good works and from people in desperate need so that He could slow down and replenish. In our culture of busy, busy, busy, we are often so preoccupied with ourselves and our lives that we are unable to be fully present with the God of the universe. We allow our busyness to migrate into our souls. That, my friend, is too busy!

It is our job to create the space our soul needs (see Psalm 23:1–3). When we create space through journaling for the soul, God grows us and replenishes us. Jesus also engaged in practices that allowed God's grace to keep replenishing His spirit. Jesus prayed. He fed His mind with Scripture. He offered thanks. He spent time hanging out with a few close friends. The practices of Jesus offer this same replenishment to our souls.

Remarkably, research shows that the benefits of these replenishing spiritual practices are increased when they are performed in conjunction with one another.

Journaling for the soul slows us down, creates for us some much-needed space, and increases the benefits to our soul of the other soul replenishing disciplines.

Journaling for the soul also provides us with many other valuable benefits:

- The physical act of writing is itself good for the brain.

- Journaling documents what God is currently teaching us (see Psalm 106).

- Our thoughts are fragmented, jumping quickly from one thing to another. Writing is a linear process that helps us find the gaps in our thinking.

- Journaling helps us "see" more clearly and gives us the ability to make connections we might not have otherwise been able to make.

- The process of journaling helps us explore our true self, unmasked.

- Research shows that we remember a very small percentage of what happens to us each day. We also forget most of our feelings and reactions. Recording them helps us remember.

- Journaling provides a record of our spiritual growth, one that we can look back on as a reminder of God's persistent work in our lives.

- Journaling for the soul gifts us with the opportunity to be creative as we use our interests and God-wiring to connect with Him.

- It blesses our loved ones with a gift of legacy.

The benefits of journaling for the soul are many, and the list could go on, but the benefits do not lie in reading *about* journaling for the soul. They lie in *doing* it.

The remainder of this handbook is devoted to just that. In the next section, you will find tips to help you get started and get the most benefit out of your journaling. The final section is filled with method sheets—lots of method sheets. There are methods of the more traditional journaling variety as well as nontraditional methods. Some methods connect with prayer, some with feeding the soul with Scripture, and some connect with other disciplines.

It does not matter which journaling method you choose. What matters is engaging with God as you care for your soul. Remember as you journal that even though you are by yourself in a quiet place, you are not alone. God, your Father, is always with you. Slow down, replenish through this fun little thing called journaling for the soul, and exhale!

May you be blessed as the time you spend with your heavenly Father becomes more intentional, consistent, and intimate. Be drawn ever closer to Him as you lean more and more into Him. Nourish your soul. **Know Him.**

Tip: Overall Journaling Success

Take baby steps. Start small and keep it simple. Don't overwhelm yourself by jumping into multiple methods at the same time. Choose one or two methods. Journaling for the soul is a discipline for a lifetime. Keep your journaling simple enough that you want to continue it.

Give yourself permission. Many, if not all, of these methods will be new to you. Give yourself permission to try some of them even if they cause a little discomfort. You won't know if you don't try. At the same time, give yourself permission to abandon anything that just simply does not work for you. Again, you won't know if you don't try, but not all methods are a fit for everyone.

Loosen up. Remember, just as there is no right or wrong way to pray, there is no right or wrong way to journal. If it works for you, it's right.

Be intentional. Setting aside time for this important discipline is key. Schedule it. Put in on your calendar. Set an alarm.

Set the tone. To receive the most benefit from your journaling, the time you set aside for it needs to be uninterrupted, quiet time, preferably when you are alone, alert, and ready.

Be consistent. As tough as it is, try to journal every day. Setting aside time to journal every day or at least once a week at a specific time sets the stage for follow-through success.

Don't catch up. While consistency is our goal and will produce the greatest benefits to our souls, there will be times we simply cannot journal on our "journaling day" or at our "journaling time." Don't allow this to cast a shadow over you. Be okay with it. Then continue on. This precious discipline is meant as a source of nourishment, growth, and joy. Don't be robbed of the blessing.

Ask yourself questions. Many of the journaling for the soul methods included in this handbook include questions. Answering those questions can help lead you to your next thought and propel you forward in your writing.

Do not give up. Starting a new habit can be difficult. In fact, research shows that depending on the behavior desired, the person involved, and the surrounding circumstances, it can take anywhere from 18 to 254 days for someone to form a new habit. Given all that is involved in the discipline of journaling for the soul, it may take a few weeks for this new habit to be formed.

Be honest. It is not always easy, but it is so very important to take time to reflect and to think about what is going on in a particular situation. God grows us in the hard places of self-reflection and honesty.

Prepare an invitation. Leave your current journal in plain view so that it can beckon you to come and spend time with God.

Date your entries. This habit is a great way to get something on your blank page, and it will help you track your spiritual growth over time. If you are away from home, it is also a good idea to jot down your location and why you are there. This will help put your journal entry into a context.

Add details. Record your mood/emotions at the time of each entry. This is also quite helpful when looking back at your entries and trying to put them into context.

Banish the editor and the art critic. This is that voice that booms from the darkest recesses of your mind such things as, "You shouldn't be writing that," "That is not the way to write," "It doesn't look like everyone else's," or "You call that art?"

Remove barriers. I tend toward perfectionism. This trait can be a paralyzing agent when it comes to journaling. Making those first few marks in a journal can be traumatic. What if I mess up the page? To get around this obstacle, I have developed the practice of purchasing inexpensive composition notebooks for my journaling adventures. These books can typically be found for about one dollar. Even better than that, during back to school season I have been able to pick them up for fifty cents each. Using these books moves me beyond the paralysis. I'm not quite so upset if I spill something on it or "mess it up" in some way.

Reread. Establish a practice of reading your entries at a later time—after a short break, at the end of the day, or even at the end of a week, month, or year.

Reflect. When you re-read an entry, consider adding an insight line. An insight line is a brief reflective sentence or two. What is God teaching you? What question do you still have? How have you grown? What new insight do you now have?

Re-evaluate from time to time. Whether it's at the beginning of each new month, on your birthday, or at New Year's, plan for a time to reflect on your current journaling method(s). If the method is no longer working for you, change it. For added insight, whenever you choose to leave a method behind, either temporarily or permanently, take the opportunity to record the "why" in your journal.

Mix it up. Many of the methods shared in this book can be incorporated into other disciplines. There are no rules or limits. Take for example Verse Mapping, which is a method for Scripture journaling. Try using it as you pray and call it prayer mapping. Or use it when journaling your spiritual journey and call it spiritual journey mapping.

Stay with it. Journaling for the soul is a discipline that requires perseverance. When its newness wears off, when you don't feel like it, when you are going through the "hard," press on. Ask God for His help and strength and energy to keep going in this worthwhile endeavor.

Tip: Choosing a Method

Remember, start small and keep it simple. You don't want to overwhelm yourself to the point of giving up. Begin by choosing one journaling for the soul method to engage in.

In order to decide which method is best for you right now, ask yourself some questions:

1. **For what purpose do I want to journal in this season of my life?**

   ☐ Digging into Scripture ☐ Preaching truth to myself

   ☐ Prayer ☐ To learn more about a specific topic

   ☐ Thanksgiving/gratitude ☐ To turn my focus toward Christ

   ☐ Praise ☐ To unpack sermon notes

   ☐ Self-reflection

2. **Which method is most "doable" for me right now?**

3. **Am I drawn to the more traditional styles or the non-traditional ones?**

4. **Is there a particular format I would like to try?**

   ☐ Side-by-side pages ☐ Letters

   ☐ Conversation ☐ Artsy

   ☐ List

5. **Do I see a particular method that I "just have" to try?**

   ☐ Color Coded Journaling ☐ Praying in Color Journaling

   ☐ Evidences of Grace Journaling ☐ "Self-Counsel" Journaling

   ☐ Love Letters to God Journaling ☐ Verse Mapping Journaling

Tip: Journaling within a Particular Spiritual Discipline

Digging into Scripture

1. Strategically choose passages of Scripture for journaling:

- Choose a book of the Bible you want to learn more about.

- Select a well-known passage you are interested in, such as the Sermon on the Mount, the Lord's Prayer, or the Birth of Christ.

- Focus in on a single chapter; for example, any one of the Psalms, Romans 8, or 1 Corinthians 13.

- Scripture journal your sermon notes.

- Dig deeper into a current or past Bible study, your personal devotion, small group, or Sunday school materials.

- Use Scripture challenges. These can be found via a Google or Pinterest search. Try Scripture Challenges, Bible Reading Challenges/Plans, or Scripture Writing Challenges when you search.

2. Write Scriptures you are studying on 3x5 note cards and carry them with you. Pull them out for review or reflection during down times.

3. Use your phone to snap a photo of your Scripture or journaling page. Pull it up when waiting in the car line or doctor's office. Having it on your phone can be more convenient at times than carrying a 3x5 card. Plus, if you photograph your full journal page, you have access to the thoughts and reflections you recorded, as well as the Scripture.

4. Use your phone's text feature. Text the Scripture to yourself or text reminders to review the Scripture.

5. Post the day's Scripture on your social media accounts for easy access throughout the day.

Prayer

1. Write out your prayers.

2. Use one color to record your prayer requests and another color to record the answers.

3. Celebrate answers and praises.

Self-Reflection

1. Do self-reflective journaling on a regular basis:

- Write re-visit dates on your calendar or set a phone alarm.

- Associate your follow-ups with a recurring date: first of each month, your birthday, New Year's Day.

2. Be honest! Self-reflection can be hard, but it's in these places that God grows us best.

Soul Searching

1. Jot down daily what is going on in your life.

2. Record yearly check points and reflect on spiritual growth in examined areas.

3. Be honest! God already knows, and He offers grace upon grace.

Tip: Personalizing Your Journal

The methods in this handbook are wide and varied. Each is a powerful tool for helping you connect with God, nourish your soul, and grow spiritually. They are intended as a help. Let them jump-start you and spur you on, but don't allow them to limit you. Over time, you should begin to develop your own style.

Keep in mind that the steps given for each method are provided as suggestions. Permit them to inspire you. If and when you are comfortable, leave their confines and venture out. Adjust the methods to fit your liking. Mix them up or combine them. Who knows? You might even create something entirely different from the methods on these pages.

Let it happen. Be as creative as you want. You are a child of the Creator. He wired you. Try using your interests, gifts, and talents as you engage with Him via your journal. Play with stickers, doodle, use photographs, or explore words. Be drawn to Him through the things you enjoy. What greater way to glorify Him than by using the unique wiring He gifted to you.

Make your journal your own:

- Keep a ready supply of pencils, pens, highlighters, and colored pencils near your journal for easy access.

- Highlight, enlarge, underline, frame or bold words that stand out to you as important.

- Add color for visual appeal.

- Create a color-coding system.

- Doodle symbols to clarify deep doctrine.

- Draw pictures to add your personality to your entries.

- Use stickers, rubber stamps, and paint.

- Write out your questions and thoughts when they come to you. Write them right there on your page as part of your entry.

- Record references (chapter, verse, author, speaker, etc.) for future reference.

- Hold on to Bible study, conference, workshop, and sermon notes on topics that interest you. Use them for future journaling.

A COLLECTION OF
Journaling
METHODS

Prayer
Journaling

Prayer is simply conversing with God about what we are experiencing and about what, together with Him, we are doing. Prayer is a way of life. It is important that we think of prayer, not as mustering up energies and words, but as joining in with God's activity. Prayer is opening our lives to God and acknowledging our total dependence on Him.

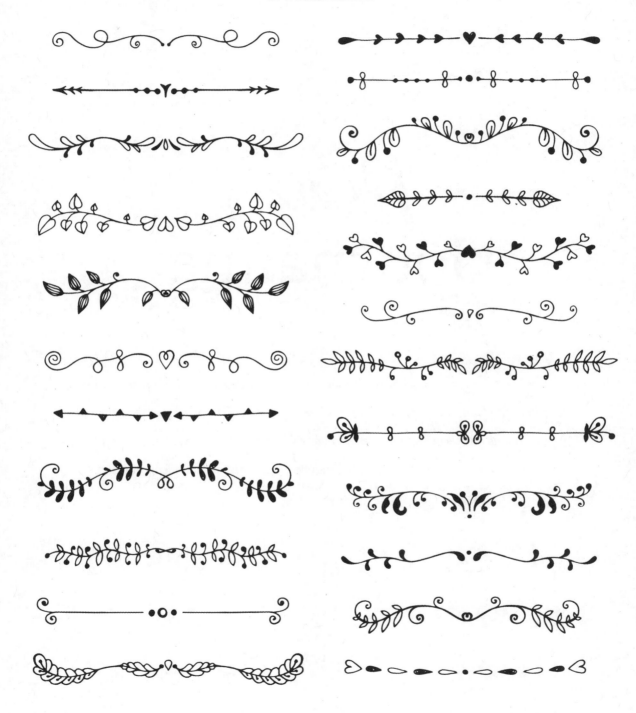

Lectio Divina Journaling

Lectio Divina is a traditional method of Bible reading and prayer aimed at encouraging communion with God. On occasion, this spiritual discipline is confused with the *lectio divina* of Eastern mysticism, which is an emptying of the mind. As a spiritual practice, *Lectio Divina* is actually quite the opposite. It is the *filling* of your mind with a verse, passage, or truth of God and letting it soak in deeply.

Lectio Divina journaling is simply the process of recording your thoughts, reflections, and findings as you apply this method to your Bible reading.

Materials:

- Blank journal or composition book
- Pen or pencil
- Bible verse, passage, or truth

Method:

Step 1: Choose your passage and read through it thoughtfully. Read it multiple times.

Step 2: Ask questions and record the answers in your journal:
  › What does the text say?
  › What is going on in this Bible passage?
  › What is the context?

Step 3: To gain a better understanding of the context, use a Bible commentary and/or cross references.

Step 4: Meditate on the passage. Meditating simply means to "think on" the verse. Ask yourself, "What is God saying to me through the text?"

Step 5: Pray. Talk to God about the text. Tell Him your feelings. Be honest; God can handle any emotions that you have. Share what you have learned. Ask for His help in applying it to your life. Read the Scripture in an attitude of prayer.

Step 6: Take action. How should knowing the truth of this Scripture affect your life?

Legacy Prayer Journaling

A Legacy Prayer Journal is kept by members of multiple generations within a family. The journal is typically sectioned off by categories such as prayer requests and answers to prayer.

This type of prayer journal encourages modeling and discussion of prayer. It also becomes a treasured family keepsake and a record of God's movement within your family.

Materials:

- Blank journal, composition book, or three-ring binder filled with loose-leaf paper and tabbed dividers

- Pen or pencil

- Optional: Anything else you want to include in your family's legacy journal

Method:

Step 1: Set up your journal. Decide on the categories you would like to include. Consider these possibilities:

> - Prayer requests

> - Answers to prayer

> - What I am learning

> - Favorite Scriptures

> - We are grateful for

> - Anything your family chooses

Step 2: As a family, determine how and when entries will be made into the journal and who will be in physical possession of it.

Long-distance grandparents can keep a legacy prayer journal with their children and grandchildren by using technology to share requests and gather information.

Step 3: Use your legacy prayer journal as a tool for sharing requests, praises, and other important information among family members. From time-to-time, pull it out for a sweet time of reflection and discussion during family gatherings.

Picture Prayer Journaling

A Picture Prayer Journal is made up of photographs. These are used as prayer prompts and a connection point to the person being prayed for. Picture prayer journals work well as tools when praying for your children, grandchildren, students, or others.

Materials:

- Blank journal, composition book, or three-ring binder filled with loose-leaf paper and tabbed dividers
- Pen or pencil
- Photograph of each person you want to include
- Adhesive
- Optional: Anything else you wish to include in your journal

Method:

Step 1: Set up your journal. This type of journal is set up by person rather than category. If using a blank journal or composition book, begin by dividing the total number of pages in your journal by the number of people you will be adding to your journal. This will help you determine how many pages to reserve for each person.

Step 2: For each person, place their name and birthdate in an upper corner of the first page of their section.

Step 3: Attach a small photo of the person.

Step 4: Use the remainder of the pages to record prayers, prayer requests, praises, answers to prayers, notes, and anything else you like.

Pray the Alphabet Journaling

The alphabet can be a powerful tool for engaging with God. Some of the psalmists of the Bible used letters of the alphabet termed an Acrostic to begin the verses of their psalms. I often use the alphabet as I spend time alone with God to praise, to offer thanks, and to make requests.

Materials:

- Blank journal or composition book
- Pen or pencil

Method:

Step 1: Pray the alphabet. Work your way from A to Z:

> › For others by name
> › Through the list of godly characteristics you wish to exhibit in your own life or see exhibited in the lives of your children and/or grandchildren
> › For your government leaders, states, or countries
> › Through Bible verses, chapters, or the promises of God
> › Through God's character or attributes
> › In thanksgiving or praise

Step 2: Record your prayers or the things you pray in your journal.

Praying in Color Journaling

In her book, *Praying in Color: Drawing a New Path to God*, Sybil MacBeth explains that Praying in Color is both process and product.[1] A unique prayer technique, its benefits are many. Two of my favorite benefits are the stimulated engagement and sustained focus produced during prayer as a result of the constant hand movement of the person praying. Additionally, Praying in Color offers a concrete way to pray (process), as well as a visual record of that prayer (product).

Materials:

- Journal or a blank sheet of paper
- Pen, fine-tip Sharpie, any black roller ball pen
- Colored markers, colored pencils, colored gel pens

Method:

Step 1: Write the name of the person you are praying for on a sheet of paper. Draw any shape around the name or simply begin to doodle around it.

Step 2: Continue to add marks and shapes. Focus on the person as you do. Ask God to be part of your prayer time. If words come, pray them. If they do not, enjoy sitting in silence with God on behalf of the person.

Step 3: After a few minutes or as the Holy Spirit leads, move on in your prayer. Choose a specific need, verse of Scripture, character virtue, or anything else you want to pray for that person. Write this in another area of your paper. Pray as you draw around it, adding more color and doodles.

Step 4: Continue to add other specifics, such as Scriptures or virtues, to your prayer. Pray for each as it pertains to the person. Each time a detail is added to your prayer, embellish it with color and doodles as you pray.

Additional Notes:

> There is no time limit. Adjust each prayer to the amount of time you have available and move along through your prayer as the Spirit leads.

> There is no right or wrong way to pray in color. These steps are intended as a helpful starting point. No artistic talent or ability is required.

> Praying in Color can be adapted to any type of prayer: thanksgiving, intercession, praise, or adoration.

1. Sybil MacBeth, *Praying in Color: Drawing a New Path to God* (Brewster, MA: Paraclete Press, 2013), 5.

Scripture Prayer Journaling

Praying Scripture is a powerful way to shape your thoughts and petitions when talking with God. As you pray Scripture, the words of the Bible become your words. Not only are you equipped with *what* to pray, you can *know* that what you are praying is God's will. Additionally, praying Scripture helps you learn and treasure God's Word, eases your anxiety, and draws you closer to God.

Materials:

- Blank journal or composition book
- A favorite pen or pencil
- Scripture passage of choice

Method:

Step 1: *Select Your Passage.* To begin your journey of praying Scripture, start with relatively short and familiar passages. Be sure you understand the context and meaning of the passage.

Good places to begin are the book of Psalms; Joshua 1:9; 2 Corinthians 12:9–10; Ephesians 1:15–23; Ephesians 3:14–21; Philippians 1:9–11; Colossians 1:3–14; James 1:5–8, or any passage that has special meaning to you.

Step 2: *Read Your Passage.* Read over your passage several times before beginning to pray. You might even choose to read it in another translation or two as well. This will help with your understanding of the passage and make choosing the words of your prayer easier.

Step 3: *Pray Your Passage.* As you pray, write out your prayer in your journal. Consider writing your journal entry in the form of a letter. Begin by addressing the Lord as you would with any other prayer: Heavenly Father; Dear Jesus; Oh Lord, etc. Then, simply go through the passage line by line, phrase by phrase, talking to God about whatever comes to your mind as you read. Another option is to read your passage word-for-word in an attitude of prayer.

Squish-It Prayer Journaling*

Squish-It Prayer Journaling is a twist on the popular *Smash Journals* by K&Company. To get an idea of this journaling method, think journal, scrapbook, and doodle pad all rolled into one—with no set plan. (I will admit the no set plan was difficult for me at first as my personality naturally wanted to organize each page around a topic, but in time I managed to get over it.)

The Squish-It Journal is a place to squish in all manner of things that bring God to your mind, remind you of His love and care, and encourage you. It is also a place to write Scripture, prayers, quotes, lists, and anything else. The journals are fun, easy to create, and can be continually added to. My favorite thing about them, though, is the way they kindle communication with God.

Materials:

- Blank journal or composition book
- Various adhesives: glue stick, scrapbook mounts, washi tape, staples, etc.
- A collection of things you love: quotes; Scripture; prayers; Pinterest images; things cut from magazines, church bulletins, programs, calendars, and such
- Embellishments: assorted papers, stamps, stickers, washi tape, scrapbook doodads, pens, and markers
- Other ideas: envelopes, index cards, file tabs, paint sample strips

Method:

Step 1: Decorate the cover of your journal if you choose. Then, simply begin squishing some of your favorite things into your blank journal. Go ahead, just randomly slap your items into your book. Do not plan! Don't over think!

Step 2: Set aside some time to journal by adding more items to your book. Glue items in, write in things, or decorate the pages. Make it you!

Step 3: As you feel led, when you go to prayer, grab your Squish-It Journal and sit quietly with God. Open the book, randomly turn its pages, and let your eyes fall on the items within. Talk to God about what comes to your mind as you linger over the items.

* Variations of this journaling method abound. Some of the other names I was able to track down on Pinterest and Etsy are: Smash Prayer Journals, Smash-It Prayer Journals, Junk Prayer Journals, and Smash Scripture Journals.

Scripture Journaling

Scripture Journaling *as a spiritual practice is engaging with the Bible as a means of connecting with the Person that Scripture proclaims. This practice includes the very familiar spiritual discipline of reading the Bible. It also includes: Studying the Word; Memorizing Scripture; Meditating on Scripture; Praying God's Word; Attending an organized Bible study.*

Tools for Digging Deeper into Scripture

Tools:

Commentary: A commentary is an explanation of Scripture written by one person or a group of people. It is broken down either verse-by-verse or by a complete passage. A commentary is *interpretation* of biblical text. It expands the biblical text, but it is not the translation of the original manuscripts.

Concordance: A concordance is a reference tool for studying the Bible. It is made up of word lists and formatted in alphabetical order. Under each word entry is a list of verses where that word can be located. A concordance shows where words appear throughout Scripture and is useful when doing a *specific word study* across Greek, Hebrew, and English.

Cross-reference: A cross-reference is a verse that has a similar (related) theme or topic as the verse that you are reading. Many Bibles include cross-references directly on the Bible text page. Cross-references can also easily be found using a Bible-help website. Cross-referencing is a way to use Scripture in order to interpret Scripture. Simply search other verses that reference the same themes, words, events, or people as the passage you are reading to gain a deeper understanding.

Bible websites:

Blue Letter Bible: Blue Letter Bible provides powerful tools for an in-depth study of God's Word through a free online reference library, with study tools that are grounded in the historical, conservative Christian faith. Visit the Blue Letter Bible website at https://www.blueletterbible.org/.

YouVersion: YouVersion is a free Bible on your phone, tablet, and computer. The Bible app allows users to read the Bible, share verses with their social networks, bookmark their favorite passages, and more. Visit YouVersion at https://www.youversion.com/.

Color-Coded Journaling

Color coding is the process of marking the words of a text by color. This process requires the reader to read at a slow pace and requires thought. Color coding also allows the reader to see patterns and themes in the Bible more easily, and it's pretty.

Color-Coded Journaling can easily be done one of two ways. The first way is to print out the selected Bible text using a computer, color code the printout, and then place the completed sheets in a binder, creating a journal. The second way is to write the selected Scripture by hand in a journal or composition book and then color code the written text.

Color coding is such a simple method, but one that yields tremendous results. The most difficult part of the entire process is deciding upon your coding system. Don't let that stop you. If it seems overwhelming, begin with a simple two or three-color code.

Materials:

- Blank journal, composition book, or computer printout of Scripture text
- Coloring tools: colored pencils, colored ink pens, Crayola Twistables, etc.
- Color Coding Chart (Numerous charts can be found via a Google or Pinterest search OR create your own)
- Optional: straight edge or ruler

Method:

Step 1: Choose a passage of the Bible to examine more closely through color coding.

Step 2: Decide what color coding chart you will use. You might start by doing a quick internet search for coding charts. Choose one from your search results or create your own by combining ideas from your search results with your own personal preferences.

Step 3: Gather your materials and get started!

Step 4: Using your chart, mark the words of the Bible text by color.

Variations:

› Add other marks: circle powerful words or phrases; underline words or phrases you do not understand; draw arrows when you make connections to the text, ideas, or experiences; list arguments, important ideas, or key points.

› Read any or all of the Letters of Paul. Use three colors for coding: one for every occurrence of FAITH within the text, one for HOPE, and one for LOVE.

Create a Color Code

☐ Names / Attributes of God   ☐ _____

☐ Christ / Redemption   ☐ _____

☐ Holy Spirit / Truth / Light   ☐ _____

☐ God the Father   ☐ _____

☐ God's Commands   ☐ _____

☐ Warnings   ☐ _____

☐ Negative Consequences   ☐ _____

☐ Evil   ☐ _____

☐ Heavenly Hope   ☐ _____

☐ People / Places / Numbers   ☐ _____

☐ Prophecies   ☐ _____

☐ Promises   ☐ _____

☐ Miracles   ☐ _____

☐ Belief   ☐ _____

☐ Identity in Christ   ☐ _____

☐ Praise   ☐ _____

"A Little Bit of Everything" Scripture Journaling

This type of journaling is pretty much as it sounds: It is a freestyle type of Scripture journaling that combines several different types of your preferred methods.

Recently, after conducting a ladies' retreat on *Journaling Across the Disciplines*, I received a phone call from one of the participants. She was so excited about what she had learned and was already using, she just had to share. She shared about creating prayer journals for her grandchildren, about Praying in Color for a teen at her church, and about how she was digging into Scripture by combining several of the journaling methods she had been introduced to at the retreat.

Materials:

- Blank journal or composition book
- Pen or pencil
- Selected portion of Scripture (Psalm 23, Psalm 34, 1 Corinthians 13, The Lord's Prayer, The Sermon on the Mount, The Parable of the Soils, or any favorite passage)
- Colored pencils, colored pens, markers
- Computer images, magazines
- Adhesive
- Optional: washi tape, stamps and stamp pads, stickers, any other art or scrapbooking supplies

Method:

Step 1: Write out the text of your selected Scripture on the right-hand pages of only your journal. Be sure to skip one or two lines as you write, leaving plenty of white space.

Step 2: Add your thoughts, reflections, and questions on the corresponding left-hand pages or in the white space surrounding the text.

Step 3: Do an internet search on your Scripture passage. Collect your favorite resulting images, quotes, and other gems. Add them to your journal.

Step 4: Pray in Color any of the verses you choose.

Step 5: Examine some of the verses more closely by verse-mapping them (see page 64).

Step 6: Look for recurring words in the passage. Do a word study.

Step 7: Pray all or a portion of your Scripture.

Step 8: Share highlights of your study with others via social media, email, or in person.

Note: These "steps" are meant more as suggestions and ideas. Add to them. Take away from them. Mix up the order. The study is yours. Do the steps that fit your passage, your personality, and your season.

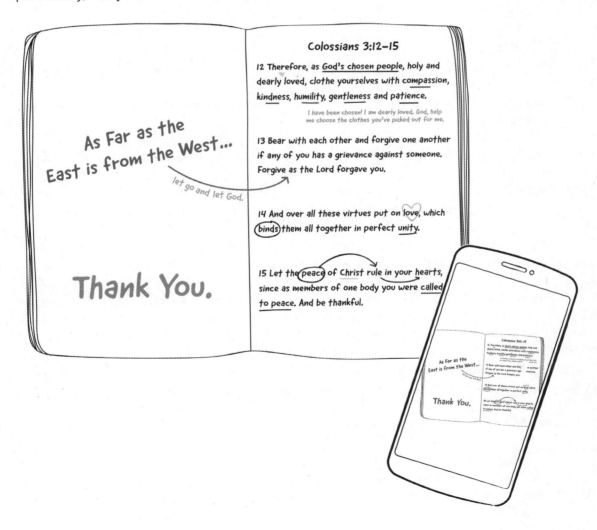

Biographical Study Journaling

Recall from your elementary school days that a biography is a written account of another person's life. Biographical Study Journaling is an effective tool to use when you desire to gain greater insight into a person of the Bible.

Materials:

- Blank journal or composition book
- Bible tools: concordance, cross-references, Bible-help websites, etc.
- Pen or pencil
- Bible

Method:

Step 1: *Write* the name of your person from the Bible at the top of your journal page.

Step 2: *List References.* Use your concordance and cross-references to find all the verses you can about this person.

Step 3: *Record* basic information and your first impressions from the text(s).

Step 4: *Create a Chronological Outline* of the person's life or time period. It is not necessary to include every little detail; major events will suffice.

Step 5: *Gain Insight.* Using the text(s) and any additional resources you choose, *look deeper* into the person's reputation, responses, and relationships.

Step 6: *Identify Character Qualities.* List the character qualities (both positive and negative) you find over the course of your multiple readings. Be sure to include references for possible use later.

Step 7: *Summarize Lessons.* Look for and record biblical truths and lessons from your study of this person. Write a short summary of what you learned.

Step 8: *Apply.* Ask God for help in discerning how to apply what you have learned to your life.

Note: Be creative in setting up your page(s), incorporating symbols and sketches to your notes if you choose. Or, keep it more traditional by simply heading sections and taking notes in list form.

Book Study Journaling

Book Study Journaling is for those times when you want to dig into a book of the Bible as a whole unit, rather than examining in it smaller bits.

Materials:

- Blank journal or composition book
- Pen or pencil
- Bible (A study Bible is particularly useful for this method)
- Bible tools: concordance, cross references, Bible help websites, etc.

Method:

Step 1: *Read it.* Read the entire book you selected in one sitting if at all possible. Then, in order to get the most benefit from your study, do this another time or two before moving on to the next step.

Step 2: *Note it.* In your journal, note the themes, style (author's word choice, sentence structure, figurative language, etc), key words, and key verses.

Step 3: *Study it.* Using your study Bible or Bible tools, find out more about the book.

> › Who is the author?
> › When was the book written?
> › Where was the book written?
> › To whom was it written? Why?

Step 4: *Outline it.* Yes, old-school style, point by point.

Step 5: *Apply it.* Determine how the book applies to you.

Note: If you want to be creative in your journaling, you might choose to divide your journal page(s) into four large sections with room for subsections. If you would rather take a more traditional approach, simply head each section or subsection as you work.

Spiritual Journaling for the Busy and Distracted

There are many effective and engaging journaling methods for digging deeper into God's Word. Book Study Journaling (p. 45), *Journible* Journaling (p. 53), and Verse Mapping (p. 64) are just a few; however, many of these methods take time—something many of us simply do not have on a daily basis or during certain seasons of our lives.

For those days and seasons when time is scarce, my friend, Betsy de Cruz, uses the method of "Spiritual Journaling for the Busy and Distracted."[2]

Materials:

- Blank journal, composition book, or index card
- Pen or pencil
- Verse of Scripture

Method:

Step 1: Write out one verse of Scripture.

Step 2: Read the verse over several times, thoughtfully.

Step 3: Choose one of the two options listed.

Option 1: Write a one-sentence prayer in your journal or on your card. Respond to what God is saying to you through your chosen verse. Your sentence can be a prayer of thanks, a request, a reflection, a question, a praise, anything.

Option 2: Choose a word. After reading the verse several times, hone in on one word that sums it up. Write the word down. Ask God what He wants to say to you. Jot down one or two thoughts that come to mind.

Step 4: Converse with God throughout your day, using your sentence prayer or your one word.

---

2. Betsy de Cruz, "When You Want More out of Time with God," *Faith Spilling Over* (blog), May 24, 2018, http://faithspillingover.com/2015/07/07/when-you-want-more-out-of-time-with-god/#more-2401. Visit Betsy's blog for other prayer, journaling, and Bible study tips.

CliffsNotes Journaling

Most of us are familiar with CliffsNotes,[3] which were originally launched by Clifton Keith Hillegass in 1958. Perhaps you even used them as you studied the works of Shakespeare or read John Milton's *Paradise Lost*. CliffsNotes are study guides that present and explain literature in an abbreviated, easy-to-understand form.

Gain a better understanding of Bible chapters and passages by CliffsNotes Journaling the important points in the chapters and passages you select.

Materials:

- Blank journal or composition book
- Pen or pencil
- Optional: colored pens, colored pencils, markers, washi tape, stickers, etc.

Method:

Step 1: In keeping with the abbreviated style of CliffsNotes, plan for each of your chapters or passages to fit on a single page.

Step 2: Select your passage. Read straight through it a couple of times to get the main idea.

Step 3: Read it again slowly and thoughtfully.

Step 4: Record the main ideas and important points on your journal page.

Step 5: Have fun and make it as pretty as you choose.

Variation: Turn your CliffsNotes Journaling up a notch by journaling an entire book such as Ruth or Ephesians, chapter by chapter.

---

3. Clifton Keith Hillegass, *CliffsNotes*, acquired by Houghton Mifflin Harcourt, 2012, https://www.cliffsnotes.com.

5 Ws and 1 H (5W1H) Journaling

Who? What? When? Where? Why? And How? are questions whose answers are considered basic in the gathering of information or solving of a problem. These six questions are often mentioned in journalism, research, and police investigations. They constitute a formula for getting the complete story on a given subject.

Materials:

- Blank journal or composition book
- Pen or pencil
- Bible

Method:

Step 1: Gather your materials and select a passage or book of Scripture.

Step 2: Read your passage all the way through, several times.

Step 3: Get the complete story by answering these six basic questions in your journal. Who? What? When? Where? Why? How?

Step 4: Write your answers in any format you choose:

> simple list

> single sentences

> paragraphs

> pages

MATTHEW 6:19-21

"Do not store up for yourselves treasures on earth, where moths and vermin destroy, and where thieves break in and steal. But store up for yourselves treasures in heaven, where moths and vermin do not destroy, and where thieves do not break in and steal. For where your treasure is, there your heart will be also.

WHO: Jesus was speaking to his disciples and the crowd of people that were following him.

WHAT: This is a portion of Jesus' "sermon on the mount."

WHEN: Jesus spoke this early in his ministry when he first called the disciples.

WHERE: On a mountainside in Galilee.

WHY: Jesus is telling us to keep our hopes in eternal things and not earthly things.

HOW: By keeping my priorities straight and always seeking His Kingdom first.

Digging Deeper Journaling

Digging Deeper Journaling is a systematic Bible study method. When surface reading just isn't enough, when you just need to know more, "dig deep."

Materials:

- Blank journal or composition book
- Pen or pencil
- Bible
- Bible tools: concordance, cross-references, Bible-help websites
- Digging Deeper Journaling Guide (located on the following page)

Method:

Step 1: Record the passage you are studying at the top of your new journal page.

Step 2: Use the Digging Deeper Guide to help you study the passage. Be sure to record your discoveries, insights, reflections, thoughts, and questions in your journal as you work.

> › *Dig Around.* Familiarize yourself with the chapter or passage.
> › *Dig In.* Find out more about the chapter or passage.
> › *Dig Beyond.* Focus on discovering more within the chapter or passage.
> › *Dig Deeper.* Go further still into the chapter or passage.

Digging Deeper Journaling Guide

Dig Around (Familiarize)

☐ Read through the passage at a normal pace.

☐ Read it again, this time deliberately. Note any verses or ideas that seem to jump out at you.

☐ Answer: Who wrote this passage? To whom? What were the circumstances surrounding the writing?

☐ Optional: Select a verse to memorize. Write it in your journal and on an index card to post or carry with you.

Dig In (Find Out More)

☐ Print out the chapter or copy it onto the right-hand pages of your journal.

☐ Look for and mark repeated words, phrases, or ideas.

☐ Look up and write out word definitions and/or synonyms.

☐ Make lists of important information, common characteristics, or anything of interest.

☐ Draw a picture.

☐ Locate cross references.

☐ Ask questions.

☐ Optional: Choose a verse to Verse Map or to Pray in Color.

Dig Beyond (Focus)

☐ Record any truths, promises, commands, or instructions from the passage.

☐ Use physical or online resources to learn more about the Scripture.

☐ In your journal, outline or diagram the passage.

☐ Create a timeline of the events in the passage.

☐ Answer: What is God teaching me in this passage? How does this apply to my life now?

☐ Optional: Choose a portion of the Scripture: Illustrate it or paraphrase it.

Dig Deeper (Further)

☐ Answer: What does this chapter or passage reveal to me about God's character?

Dig Deeper (Still) by choosing one or more of the following:

(Not all of these options will fit with every passage.)

☐ Summarize what you have learned.

☐ Create a list of 3-5 truths or values to be shared with others.

☐ Compare and contrast important ideas from the Scripture.

☐ Become one of the people in your passage for a few minutes, and write a diary entry as that person.

☐ Write a letter to any biblical character from your passage.

☐ Write a letter to God in response to the Scripture.

☐ Compose a poem or song based upon this passage.

☐ Write out key verses as prayers.

☐ Share what you have learned with a soul friend, your husband, an acquaintance, or on social media.

Inductive Study Journaling

According to the Merriam-Webster Dictionary, "inductive" means employing mathematical or logical reasoning.[4] And while there are many forms of this system to be found and many prominent names (both individuals and organizations) attached to them, I am unsure that anyone can claim to be the originator as people in the fields of logic and mathematics have been using systems of "inductive" questioning as far back as Plato.

Inductive Bible Study is an intentional way of digging into Scripture. It involves moving from a place of looking at the evidence in and around the biblical text to a place of drawing conclusions regarding the meaning of passages and books.

Materials:

- Blank journal or composition book
- Pen or pencil
- Bible: selected passage of Scripture

Method:

Step 1: Write out your passage beginning at the top of your journal page.

Step 2: Read through the passage a time or two to become familiar with it.

Step 3: In your journal, answer the following:

> › What does the text say? [Observation]
>
> › What does the text mean? [Interpretation]
>
> › How does God want me to live in light of the truth of His Word? [Application]

Step 4: Date your page.

---

4. Merriam-Webster Dictionary Online, s.v. "Inductive," accessed May 30, 2018, https://www.merriam-webster.com/dictionary/inductive.

Journible Journaling

Journible is a fairly "new-on-the-scene" method of Scripture study based on Deuteronomy 17:18. The series of books by this name was developed by Rob Wynalda.[5] The process of *Journible* invites you to write out a chosen book of the Bible on the right-hand page of your journal and then to record your thoughts, insights, and reflections about the Scripture on the corresponding left-hand page. The physical act of writing required with *Journible* is good for the brain and increases retention. The process slows one down and promotes hiding God's Word in your heart. But the greatest benefits I have found to this method of journaling/study are increased conversation with God about His Word and a deepened relationship with Him.

Materials:

- Blank journal or composition book
- Pen or pencil
- Bible book of choice
- Optional: highlighter, colored pens or pencils, etc.

Method:

Step 1: Gather your materials and select the book of the Bible you would like to study.

Step 2: On the right-hand pages of your journal only, write out the first chapter of the book. Write your text on every other line of the page, leaving at least one line of space to provide additional room for your observations and notations.

Step 3: Sit down with the handwritten Scripture. As you read it thoughtfully, record your thoughts, reflections, insights, and questions on the corresponding left-hand page.

You decide: Write out the entire book before engaging with it in focused thought, or write and reflect in smaller chunks of text.

Ideas for starting: Begin with a small book such as 1 John, Ephesians, or Galatians. If even a small book seems overwhelming or you just want to "test the waters" with *Journible,* try the method with a single chapter, such as Psalm 34, 63, or 100.

Note: The *Journible* method is a great fit with book study journaling. Consider combining the two.

5. Rob Wynalda, *Journibles: The 17:18 Series* (Grand Rapids: Reformation Heritage Books, 2009–2015). The author's books can be found on several websites, including amazon.com, christianbook.com, and heritagebooks.org.

Praying Scripture in Color Journaling

Praying in Color, from the book *Praying in Color: Drawing a New Path to God,* is a unique prayer technique developed by Sybil MacBeth,[6] but don't be fooled into thinking it can only be used for prayer. Many of the methods discussed in *Journaling for the Soul* can be used in multiple ways and for multiple purposes. Praying in Color is no exception. Reap its benefits of deeper engagement and increased focus as you spend time with Scripture. The process will provide a concrete way to meditate on Scripture while the product will be a visual record of the time spent.

Materials:

- Journal or a blank sheet of paper
- Pen, fine-tip Sharpie, any black roller ball pen
- Colored markers, colored pencils, colored gel pens

Method:

Option 1: Write your chosen verse of Scripture on a sheet of paper or on your journal page. Meditate on the verse by reading it over and over, either aloud or in your head. Talk with God about what the verse means. As you spend time with the Scripture and with God, keep your pencil moving by adding color and design to your page.

Option 2: Write out your Scripture verse. Spend some time quietly reading over the verse several times. Ask God to give you a word or a phrase. Then circle the word or phrase that jumps out at you. (If nothing jumps out, simply choose.) Next, concentrate your meditation, prayer, color, and design on that word or phrase. What is God revealing to you about how that word relates to other words in the passage? What is He revealing to you about His character? What truth is being uncovered?

Option 3: After reading over your Scripture verse, draw out a design on a sheet of paper or in your journal. Go back to your verse. As you meditate on the verse, add its words and your thoughts, reflections, or questions to the design you drew.

6. Sybil MacBeth, *Praying in Color: Drawing a New Path to God* (Brewster, MA: Paraclete Press, 2013), 63–71.

Scripture Journaling

Scripture Journaling is a way of studying and responding to the Bible with your own words, sketches, stenciling, images, painting, stamping, or other art media.

There are many benefits to Scripture Journaling.

It is a tool for growing in grace and getting to know the heart of God through His Word.

Scripture Journaling helps move you from the act of reading the Bible for information to reading it for transformation.

Scripture Journaling can help you experience truth and discover the character of God.

Materials:

- Journaling Bible, blank journal, art book, or composition book
- Pencil
- Fine tip black ink pen
- Eraser
- Optional: colored pencils, colored markers, Crayola Twistables, stickers, stamps and stamp pads, washi tape, water colors, micron pens, scrap paper, baby wipes, any art materials you have on hand

Method:

Step 1: Gather your materials. Consider turning on some music to listen to as you journal.

Step 2: Choose a Scripture verse or passage to journal. (Your selection can come from anywhere: a current Bible study, your personal devotions, family Bible reading, sermon notes, an old favorite, song lyrics, an internet search. The possibilities are endless.)

Step 3: Read your verse thoughtfully. Ponder how you want to journal the verse:

> › Using words only
> › Writing out the verse word for word
> › Recording your thoughts about the verse
> › Combining stickers with words
> › Sketching or drawing
> › Using song lyrics

Step 4: Date your entry. It's fun to look back at your work later and to have a record of your journey.

Step 5: Have fun journaling your Scripture. Don't forget to continue meditating on your Scripture as you work.

Keep in mind that there is absolutely no right or wrong way to Scripture Journal. You cannot do it the wrong way! The idea behind Scripture Journaling is not that you create great art. In fact, you do not even have to include art. The idea is that you connect with God and His Word.

Note: If you are working in a journaling Bible, be careful not to use materials that will bleed through your pages. You can test your materials on a blank page in the back of your Bible.

Scripture Meditation Journaling

Meditating on Scripture is a powerful way to dig deeper into the Word of God. The psalmist declares, *I will meditate on your precepts and fix my eyes on your ways* (Psalm 119:15, ESV).

The term *meditation* can be confusing. It can even evoke some negative thoughts and reactions when spoken.

For the sake of clarity, the definition of meditation being used in *Journaling for the Soul* is "filling our mind with a verse or passage."

To meditate on Scripture is to sit with the Bible text and allow its words to soak in deeply.

Materials:

- Blank journal or composition book
- Pen or pencil
- Scripture verse or passage
- Dictionary, thesaurus
- Optional: More Questions for Scripture Meditation (located on page 59)

Method:

Step 1: Read through the Scripture thoughtfully, two or three times. Try reading it again, aloud.

Step 2: Write out your selected verse or passage in your journal. Be sure to include the Scripture reference. You might choose to write it across the top of your page or space it out over the entire page. Leave plenty of white space around it for your notations.

Step 3: Write out the definitions of any words that jump out at you. A standard English dictionary works wonderfully for this or look up the Greek or Hebrew.

Step 4: Use a thesaurus to write out appropriate synonyms for any words that draw your attention.

Step 5: Rewrite the verse or passage in your own words.

Step 6: Record your observations, reflections, and/or questions about this Scripture:

> › What do I notice?
>
> › How am I responding right now to this Scripture?
>
> › Is anything puzzling me?
>
> › What does this verse or passage teach me about the character of God?
>
> › How does this apply to my life?

Step 7: Write out clear and specific application points for your life. Write out a prayer about what God is teaching you in this Scripture.

Note: Make this journaling method fit you. If you have time restraints or simply want to do a deeper dive into the Scripture, only do one or two steps each day until you have worked through the entire passage.

More Questions for Scripture Meditation

Below is a library of questions for those who want to go deeper with their Scripture Meditation Journaling:

Questions for Comprehension

- What do I know about the original hearers of this passage?
- What key words or phrases are repeated?
- Are there any commands issued? What are they?
- What questions are raised? Are they answered within the passage?
- What does this Scripture teach me about God's character?
- What does this passage teach me about mankind?
- Are any specific character qualities mentioned? What are they?
- What promises are found in these verses?

Questions for Interpretation

- What are the definitions of the key words?
- Are the key words in this passage used in other passages as well? If so, does that additional usage of the key words provide helpful insights about the passage?
- What is the significance of words or phrases that are repeated?

Questions to Ask at the Application Level

- What truths do I find in this passage and how should I apply these truths to my life?
- Are there decisions I need to make? Commands I need to obey?
- How can I use this Scripture to pray for others? For myself?
- How does this Scripture instruct me regarding my relationships?
- How should the truth in this passage impact my interactions with the world around me?
- Is there a promise to claim?
- Does this passage reveal an area of disobedience in my life for which I need to repent?
- What practical steps can I take to avoid failures that are described in this passage?
- Is there an example for me to follow or avoid?
- In what ways does this Scripture prompt praise or thanksgiving?
- What is God saying to me today through this passage?

Sketch Notes Journaling

Sketch Notes Journaling is a method for examining passages of the Bible in smaller chunks. This method is particularly suited to those with drawing talents.

Materials:

- Blank journal or composition book
- Pen or pencil
- Optional: colored pens, colored pencils, markers

Method:

Step 1: Choose your chapter or passage and read it completely through at least once in order to get the main idea.

Step 2: Reread the passage, this time looking for natural breaks within it.

Step 3: Section your journal page for recording information about the smaller chunks.

Step 4: Record your identified chunks (v 1–4, v 5–11, etc.) in your journal.

Step 5: Read your passage again, one chunk at a time. Sketch the main idea for each chunk in the corresponding box/section. (If you prefer, write the main idea rather than sketching it.)

S.O.A.P. Journaling

The S.O.A.P. method is a way of digging deeper into the Bible and getting more out of your time in God's Word. S.O.A.P. stands for Scripture, Observation, Application, and Prayer. S.O.A.P. is an effective process and much has been written on it. A quick internet search will turn up a plethora of posts, videos, and examples.

Materials:

- Blank journal or composition book
- Pen or pencil
- Bible: Scripture passage of choice

Method:

Step 1: *Scripture.* Choose a Scripture to study. (For the S.O.A.P. method, it is better to keep the selection short.) Write the chosen passage across the top of a new journal page.

Step 2: *Observation.* Record observations about what stood out to you as you read the Scripture. This can be one sentence or an entire book!

- › Did something in the passage have special meaning to you?
- › What do you think God is saying to you in this Scripture?
- › Ask the Holy Spirit to teach you and reveal Jesus to you.

Step 3: *Application.* Personalize what you have read by asking yourself how it applies to you right now. Perhaps it is instruction, encouragement, or correction for a particular area of your life. Write the application in your journal.

- › How can you apply this Scripture to your life?
- › Is there action you need to take right now?

Step 4: *Prayer.* Write out a prayer to God based on what you learned and ask Him to help you apply this truth to your life. This can be as simple as asking God to help you use this Scripture, or it may be a greater insight into what He is revealing to you.

Step 5: Be sure to date your page for each S.O.A.P. entry.

Variations:

- › S.O.A.K.—Scripture, Observation, Application, Kneeling
- › S.O.A.R.—Survey, Observe, Analyze, Respond

Topical Scripture Journaling

Topical Scripture Journaling takes a different approach to journaling the Scriptures than most of the methods in this book. Most Scripture journaling is done by organizing a journal by books of the Bible, chapter, passage, or verse. Topical Scripture Journaling is organized by topic.

Admittedly, a bit of effort is required in the initial set-up of a Topical Scripture Journal, but once it's ready to go, this type of journal provides a wonderful place in which to collect everything you find regarding your chosen Bible topics.

Materials:

- Blank journal or composition book
- Pen or pencil
- Optional: divider tabs, markers, and embellishments for decorating

Set-Up:

Step 1: Number all of the pages in your journal. Be sure to number them front and back.

Step 2: Write down the total number of pages in your journal. Example: Page numbering stops at page 162. Write down 162. This may help you in deciding how many pages to allot per topic.

Step 3: Write "Table of Contents" on the top of the first two pages.

Step 4: If you want to fill your topics in before you begin journaling, go ahead and write them in on your Table of Contents. You choose whether you want them in alphabetical order or grouped by a category. You also decide how many pages to allot for each topic. This portion of the set-up is entirely up to you. Don't worry about whether you are leaving enough room for your topics. When a topic's pages run out, simply write, "Go to page #___" at the bottom of the filled-up section and continue the topic on another page in your journal. Lastly, don't forget to write the topic next to the corresponding page number in your Table of Contents.

If, however, you make the choice to write your topics in as you go, just remember each time you begin a new topic to add it to your Table of Contents.

Step 5: Write the topic of each page at the top of its assigned page. Optional: Decorate your covers inside and out.

Method:

Step 1: Topics can be added to your journal at any time. When deciding upon topics, think about:

> What is important to you in your current season of life?

> What words seem to be popping up everywhere you turn?

> What interests you?

> Spend a few days listening.

> Look at your Pinterest pins.

Step 2: Dig into your topic(s) and add to your pages. There are no rules or limits to what can be added. Consider:

> Definitions

> A list of written-out Scriptures

> Scriptures written in your own words

> Quotes on the topic

> Your personal thoughts

> Insights you have gained

> Sermon notes

> Programs from conferences & workshops

> Excerpts from books written by Christian authors

> Blog posts

> Anything you can put in a book!

> Absolutely anything can be put into your Topical Scripture Journal, so think outside the box. Include sketches, diagrams, poems, artwork, scrapbooking, or anything you enjoy!

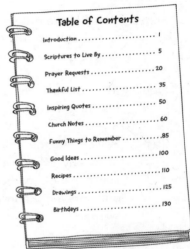

Table of Contents

Note: Remember, when it comes to methods of engaging with Scripture and journaling, there are NO rules! Your Topical Scripture Journal does not even have to be TOPICAL. Try setting one up by book of the Bible or by chapter!

Verse Mapping Journaling *

The idea behind Verse Mapping is that through the process of examining a verse more closely, you can make it yours forever.

Materials:

- Journal, composition book, paper, or index card
- Scripture verse of choice
- Pen or pencil
- Optional: highlighters, colored pens, colored pencils

Method:

Step 1: *Write.* Write out your chosen verse of Scripture. Be sure to leave plenty of white space around it, between the lines, and between the words. This will provide ample work space for your "mapping."

Step 2: *Map.* Choose any of the ideas from the Verse Mapping Guide to map your verse.

Step 3: *Review.* At the close of your mapping time or at any other time during your day, take another look at the verse. Consider writing out a prayer, sharing with God what you have learned.

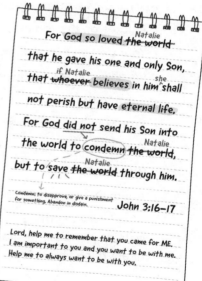

* I am not the originator of the verse mapping technique. In my search to locate its origins, I found an article on the subject at Proverbs 31 Ministries and many examples of the process at Pinterest, Google, and YouTube; however, I was unable to locate the origin.

Verse Mapping Guide

- Personalize it by crossing out pronouns such as "you," "we," and "whoever." Insert your name.

- Highlight words or phrases that jump out at you. Use different colors.

- Look up word definitions and/or synonyms.

- Read the verse in context by reading the passage, chapter, or book it is a part of.

- Read the verse in at least two other translations. Note words or phrases from other translations that help you understand or apply the verse.

- Find cross-references and note anything that brings new meaning.

- Circle a word or two and do a word study.

- Write out what you are learning.

- Record your thoughts on how you can apply the Scripture in your daily living.

Simplicity
Journaling

Simplicity *is the spiritual practice of total surrender and abandonment to God. It is having a singularity of heart or of purpose.*

For many years I lived with a misconception of simplicity. My initial reaction to the Word, even when discussed as a spiritual discipline, was to think of streamlining my life by cutting things out and getting rid of material possessions. When it comes to spiritual practices, however, simplicity means to have a singularity of heart and purpose: Jesus—the Main thing, my One thing. And, yes, this can mean having to streamline our lives if necessary in order to make Him the One thing in our life.

Evidences of Grace Journaling

Grace is defined as the unmerited favor of God toward man. In the hustle and busyness of our days, it can be easy to lose sight of His unmerited favor toward us. Evidences of Grace Journaling helps us slow down and turn our focus toward God as we record and remember His grace.

Where do you see the evidences of God's favor to you? Pay attention. Look closely. See them, for they are there.

Materials:

- Blank journal or composition book
- Pen or pencil

Method:

Step 1: *Observe.* Examine your life for evidences of God's grace. (1 Corinthians 1:4)

Step 2: *Look back.* Where do you see the work of Christ in your life? Where have you been enriched by Him in your speech and knowledge? How has God helped you, guided you, or provided for you? (1 Corinthians 1:5-6)

Step 3: *Look in.* What ongoing work is Christ doing in you? What is He teaching you? How is He growing you more and more into Christlikeness? Who is He using to speak into your life? (1 Corinthians 1:7)

Step 4: *Look forward.* How is God sustaining you to the end? What unmerited favor is He pouring out that will enable you to stand guiltless in the day of our Lord Jesus Christ? (1 Corinthians 1:8)

Note: Evidences of grace are proof of God's unmerited favor. When examining your life for evidences of His grace, guard your heart. Take care not to allow your focus to fall on the evidences (family, a relationship, success, material possessions, etc.), making idols of them. Keep your focus on the Lord, the One who covers you completely with His grace. Give Him all the praise and the glory.

Gratitude-A-Day Journaling

I will give thanks to the LORD with my whole heart; I will recount all of your wonderful deeds (Psalm 9:1, ESV).

Giving thanks to God and counting all His wonderful gifts can bring our hearts back to center. The conscious, intentional recounting can lift our eyes to Him.

Connect with your Heavenly Father. Regain your sense of wonder in the midst of life's cares. Count the beautiful gifts God is giving to you right now.

Materials:

- Blank journal, composition book, or photo journal
- Pen or pencil
- Optional: Camera

Method:

Step 1: *Set a target.* You might choose to collect a certain number of gifts or set a time frame for counting.

Step 2: *Decide* how you want to count your gifts.

> › In your journal, list a certain number of gifts each day.

> › Count gifts for twenty-six days and assign each day a letter of the alphabet. For instance, on day one, list things for which you are grateful, each one beginning with the letter "A."

> › Search the Bible for Scriptures that declare the gifts of God—salvation, grace, redemption, God's love, the Holy Spirit, etc.

> › Photograph the things for which you are thankful. Create a "Gratitude" photo journal.

Step 3: *Begin counting* the beautiful gifts God is giving to you.

Gratitude A–Z Journaling

God receives honor when we pay attention.

According to research, gratitude reaps enormous benefits. It is also shown to be a great remedy for anger, cynicism, entitlement, and other negative feelings. An often over-looked practice, gratitude is accessible to all, doesn't cost any money, and doesn't take much time. It is also nourishment for the soul. Gratitude A–Z Journaling asks us to record the things for which we are thankful—alphabetically.

Pay attention. Write it down. Worship God. Feed your soul.

Materials:

- Blank journal or composition book
- Pen or pencil

Method:

Step 1: Decide on what type of A–Z list you will be creating—a one or two-word list or something wordier.

Step 2: If your entry will be more list-like, begin by writing the alphabet down the side of your page. If you are going for something more elaborate, consider labeling as you work or leaving several lines between the letters.

Step 3: Fill in your A–Z list with the things you are thankful for.

Note: I prefer having the alphabet on the paper before I begin. My mind does not often do its best work in a linear fashion, so I find it difficult to work in A–Z order. Personally, I much prefer to add things to my already-prepared list as they come to mind.

Gratitude List Journaling

In his blog post, "10 Reasons to Be Thankful and Why You Need a Gratitude List," Jeff Goins writes, "Being grateful is a choice. So today, I choose to make a list."[7]

In their ongoing search for how we can strive to live healthy, productive lives, academic and psychological researchers have determined that practicing gratitude is near the top of the list. Peruse the mountain of blog posts, podcasts, books, or other available resources on the topic of gratitude, and you will quickly ascertain that the simple act of making a list can have a huge impact.

Materials:

- Blank journal or composition book
- Pen or pencil
- Optional: images, photographs

Method:

Step 1: Dedicate your journal or composition book to the listing of things you are grateful for.

Step 2: Decide when and how you will use your journal.

> Will you carry it with you, adding to your list throughout the day?

> Would it work better for you to keep it by your bed, recording your gratitude each night? (It is reported that even just a few minutes spent in gratitude journaling just before bed promotes nightly calm and better sleep.)

> Will you add a certain number of "gifts" each day?

> Do you want to "list" only or do you want to add your thoughts and insights to the list?

Step 3: Add "gifts" to your list daily if possible.

Note: If you want to be creative in your journaling, you might want to add images cut from magazines or photographs you have taken to the "gifts" on your list.

7. Jeff Goins, "10 Reasons to Be Thankful & Why You Need A Gratitude List," *Medium*, https://medium.com/@jeffgoins/10-reasons-to-be-thankful-and-why-you-need-a-gratitude-list-62bb68108a89.

Gratitude Prompt Journaling

According to Merriam-Webster, gratitude is "the state of being appreciative of benefits received."[8]

A quick internet search will show that it is not only Christians who espouse the powerful benefits of an attitude of gratitude. Health and science also are proclaiming its worth: lower stress levels, better sleep, focus and clarity, improved physical and psychological health, increased resilience, and so much more. Brain researchers are agreeing and adding the bold claim that genuine gratitude can physically change a person's brain for the better.

This is great news for all of us. For Christ followers, there is even more to be enjoyed: increased trust in God, a deepened relationship with Him, and the ability to see Him at work in our lives.

Grow yourself in gratitude by using topic-focused prompts as journal starters.

Materials:

- Blank journal or composition book
- Pen or pencil
- List of gratitude journaling prompts (see the following page.)

Method:

Step 1: Choose one of the journaling prompts from the list.

Step 2: Copy the prompt into your journal.

Step 3: Below the prompt, write your response.

Step 4: Date your entry.

8. Merriam-Webster Dictionary Online, s.v. "Gratitude," accessed May 31, 2018, https://www.merriam-webster.com/dictionary/gratitude.

Gratitude Prompts

Earthly Relationships:

- My spouse
- My family
- My extended family
- My soul friendships
- My friends
- My neighbors
- The hard and difficult relationships
- Broken relationships
- My pastor and his family
- Church staff
- People in positions of authority over me
- People in my life who don't know Jesus

Spiritual Blessings:

- God's lavish love
- His all-covering grace
- The beauty of His creation
- The Gospel
- Prayer
- God's sustaining provision
- He is present with me
- His power in me
- The work of the Holy Spirit in my life
- Jesus, our perfect example
- God's reign over all
- The Bible
- The attributes of God

My Identity in Christ:

- Adopted into God's family
- I am redeemed
- His workmanship
- He delights in me
- Loved unconditionally
- I am a new creation
- Washed clean

God's Demonstration of Love for Me:

- He is always with me
- God holds my hand
- He keeps a record of all my tears
- He satisfies my hunger and my thirst
- He listens to me and hears my cry

His Provision:

- Our home
- Clean water
- Food for physical nourishment
- Clothes to wear
- Care and protection
- Our physical bodies
- The "extras"

Journey toward Simplicity Journaling

We do not have to look long or hard before we come across a call to simplicity. All around us are invitations to downsize our homes, clear the clutter, and reduce unnecessary distractions.

But a much more important call to simplicity can be found in the Bible: *Servants, obey in all things your masters according to the flesh; not with eyeservice, as menpleasers; but in singleness of heart, fearing God* (Colossians 3:22, KJV). Our God is calling us to a single-minded pursuit of Himself, a purity of intention, a single focus, a complete devotion.

Journey toward Simplicity Journaling helps us develop the singular focus to which we are called. In the safety of the pages of this journal, we can remove the masks and explore the double-mindedness of our hearts.

Materials:

- Blank journal or composition book
- Pen or pencil

Method:

Step 1: Give yourself permission to let what is going on in your head come out of your mouth (or for this journaling purpose, out of your pen and onto the page). Remember: The pages of your journal offer safety, and our God offers grace.

Step 2: As you work toward a life of true biblical simplicity, record your observations, discoveries, questions, learnings, and personal reflections in your journal.

Step 3: Take what you have written in your journal to the Lord. Use your entries to spark deep, life-changing conversations with Him.

Step 4: Be sure to date your entries. This practice makes it easier to look back and see growth.

Love Letter to God Journaling

I am often reminded of a little story I heard years ago. It goes something like this:

A little boy, frightened one night during a big thunderstorm, called out to his daddy in terror, "Daddy, I'm scared!"

His father, not wanting to get out of bed, called back, "Don't worry, Son. God loves you. He is with you and will take care of you."

There was a moment of silence. Then the daddy heard his little boy say, "I know God loves me, but right now, I need somebody with skin on."

Daddy was correct. Our God is love. And loving us with His steadfast love, He never leaves us. Our Heavenly Father is limitless in His care for us even in the storms. We know this about our God. But just like the little boy, we often find ourselves in need of the tangible.

Writing love letters to God is one of those tangibles. The process allows us to take thoughts from our head and give them form on paper where our head, heart, and eyes can take them in. Beyond the tangible, engaging in the process also requires us to slow down, provides focus, draws our heart to Him, and builds our trust. Writing these letters strengthens our relationship with Him and becomes our gift of love.

Materials:

- Blank journal, composition book, or other paper
- Pen or pencil

Method:

Step 1: Find a quiet place, perhaps put on some soft instrumental music, and write your love letter to God.

Step 2: Consider writing your love letters to God on a regular basis—once a month, once a year, on your birthday.

Step 3: If kept in a journal dedicated to these love letters, the journal becomes a precious record of your relationship with God and can be used for reflection, prayer, thanksgiving, and worship.

Letter Writing Tips

- Set the mood before you begin to write.
  Don't worry about making it sound like a love letter.

- If unsure about what to write, use the format "past, present, future."

- Make it extremely personal and incredibly specific.

- Don't fret over the length, the format, or what your letter looks like.

- Write for God. Make Him your focus.

- Think about Him. What is He to you?
  List everything you appreciate and adore about Him.

- Use your memories to guide you.

- Think about the future.

"My Father" Journaling

Turn your eyes to Him. Draw closer. Dig into the Scripture and journal what you learn about your Father.

Materials:

- Blank journal or composition book
- Pen or pencil
- Bible
- Bible concordance or Bible-help website

Method:

Step 1: Gather your materials and settle into your quiet workspace.

Step 2: Use the list provided below as a starter. Add others as you dig into God's Word.

Step 3: Begin by writing out the Scripture in your journal.

Step 4: Spend time with each passage by meditating on it, Color Coding it, Praying it in Color, Verse Mapping it, or applying any journal method you choose.

My Father...

- Loves me (John 3:16)
- Cares for me (Matthew 6:26)
- Forgives me (Psalm 103:12)
- Is compassionate (Psalm 103:4–5)
- Is giving (Romans 8:32)
- Understands me (Psalm 139:1–2)
- Accepts me (Psalm 139:1–6)
- Satisfies (Psalm 107:9)
- Persistently pursues me (Luke 19:10)

- Is reasonable toward me (Isaiah 1:18)
- Pardons me (Psalm 103:3)
- Heals (Isaiah 53:5)
- Redeems me (Job 19:25)
- Is loving-kindness (Psalm 86:15)
- Renews (Isaiah 40:31)
- Is righteous (Jeremiah 9:23–24)
- Is gracious (Ephesians 1:7–8)
- Is sovereign (Psalm 103:19)

One Word for One Year Journaling

One Word for One Year Journaling is not a new idea, nor is it my original idea.

One Word Journaling is the practice of selecting a single word on which to concentrate every day for an entire year. The best word choices are those chosen for the purpose of better knowing God, our Father, and ones that will help lead us closer to Jesus Christ.

Journaling one word for one year takes the process one step further and provides a written record of the year's journey. The process is easy, uncomplicated, manageable, and simple; however, it is also a process full of meaning, definition, and transformation.

Materials:

- Blank journal or composition book
- Pen or pencil
- One Word—a word for the year
- Various collected Scriptures, quotes, images, and other media
- Optional: adhesive, colored pens/pencils, other embellishments

Method:

Step 1: Choose your word. It is a good idea to reflect on the previous year and where you are currently in your spiritual journey. Listen to others. Ask questions. All the while, bathe your choice in prayer. (For help with choosing your word, see the One Word for One Year—List of Words on the following page.)

Step 2: Over the course of the coming year, gather your findings. Collect everything you can find in connection with your word: Bible verses, quotes, sermon notes, tidbits of conversation, graphics, song lyrics, etc. Handwrite your findings into your journal or cut them out and paste them in. There is no limit other than you must be able to fit it into your journal.

Note: Throughout the year, pray. Ask God to show you what He has to teach you concerning your word as it relates to your life.

One Word for One Year—List of Words

Abandon	Different	Honor	Persistence	Silence
Abide	Diligence	Hope	Perspective	Simplicity
Abundance	Direction	Humility	Possibility	Simplify
Action	Discernment	Ignite	Power	Slow
Adapt	Disciple	Imagine	Pray	Soar
Adoration	Discipline	Integrity	Prayer	Soul
Adventure	Discover	Intention	Presence	Spirit
Alive	Embrace	Intentional	Present	Stewardship
Ambition	Empower	Invest	Progress	Stillness
Appreciate	Enjoy	Jesus	Purity	Strength
Ask	Enough	Joy	Purpose	Surrender
Awake	Faith	Kindness	Pursue	Thrive
Balance	Faithful	Kingdom	Push	Time
Battle	Family	Lead	Rebuilding	Today
Be	Father	Learn	Redemption	Together
Believe	Fearless	Less	Reduce	Tongue
Benefits	Finish	Life	Reflection	Transform
Blessing	First	Light	Relationship	Transformation
Boldness	Flourish	Link	Relax	Transition
Brave	Focus	Listen	Release	Trust
Breathe	Follow	Live	Relentless	Truth
Celebrate	Forgive	Love	Remember	Unashamed
Challenge	Forgiven	Mindfulness	Renewal	Unity
Change	Fortitude	Minimize	Resolve	Unstoppable
Choose	Forward	Momentum	Rest	Uplift
Church	Freedom	More	Restoration	Wait
Commit	Fruitful	New	Restore	Wholeness
Confidence	Generosity	No	Revel	Wisdom
Connect	Gentleness	Now	Risk	Worship
Consistent	Go	Obedience	Sabbath	Write
Content	Goodness	Open	Sacrifice	Yes
Courage	Gospel	Opportunity	Seek	Yield
Create	Grace	Optimism	Selah	
Curious	Gratitude	Organize	Self-Control	
Dare	Growth	Patience	Serve	
Deeper	Healing	Pause	Service	
Determined	Health	Peace	Shalom	
Devotion	Holy	Persevere	Shine	

Preaching the Gospel to Ourselves Journaling

Responsively Preaching the Gospel to Ourselves Journaling is a powerful tool for renewing our minds when lies fly in response to our circumstances. Two ways this can be done are with self-talk and truth journaling.

Preemptively Preaching the Gospel to Ourselves Journaling is also an essential daily practice. This form of self-preaching feeds our soul, fixes our focus, and equips us for battle. Done each morning and frequently throughout our day, this habit will remind us of the importance and power of the gospel.

Materials:

- Journal or composition book
- Pen or pencil
- Cross-centered Scriptures

Method:

Use your journal to engage with cross-centered Scriptures.

Step 1: Decide on a verse or passage to enter in your journal. Then write it in.

Step 2: Engage with the following Scripture using one of the methods in this book or come up with your own.

Scriptures on The Cross		Scriptures on Forgiveness	
1 Corinthians 15:1–3	Luke 7:36–50	Psalm 103:12	Romans 4:78
Isaiah 53:10	Luke 22:42	Psalm 130:3–4	Romans 8:1
Habakkuk 3:18	Romans 3:24–26	Isaiah 1:18	Ephesians 1:7
Matthew 28:6	Romans 6:11	Isaiah 38:17	Colossians 2:13–14
Mark 14:32–35		Isaiah 43:25	Hebrews 8:12
		Isaiah 53:6	Hebrews 10:17–18
		Micah 7:19	

Spiritual Markers Journaling

Spiritual Markers identify a time of transition, decision, or direction when you clearly know God has guided you. Recording your spiritual markers enables you, over time, to look back and see how God has faithfully directed your life according to His divine purpose.

In Joshua 4:2–7, God gives instructions to Joshua for the setting up of memorial stones. These stones were to be reminders of God's great activity in the midst of His people. These specific stones, as well as other stones and altars mentioned in the Bible, became physical markers of great spiritual encounters with God. They also provided opportunities for people to teach future generations about God's activity on behalf of His people.

Materials:

- Blank journal or composition book
- Pen or pencil

Method:

Step 1: Find a quiet place and limit distractions.

Step 2: Use any of the following questions to help bring spiritual markers to mind:

> › Do I remember the moment I became a child of God?
>
> › Have there been specific times when He called me to His ways of living?
>
> › Can I point to a time when He clearly guided me in making a decision?
>
> › Were there times when He spoke powerfully to me about a commitment I should make?
>
> › Make a list of those moments when you knew without a doubt that God was guiding you. List each as it comes to mind without regard for where it happened chronologically.

Step 3: Over the next hours, or even days, add other Spiritual Markers to your list as they come to mind.

Step 4: Review your list from time to time.

> › Use your Spiritual Markers as reminders of God's awesome power and His mighty acts on your behalf.

> › Allow this insight to give you confidence to meet new challenges and to see how God has been growing you.

> › Like the memorial stones of Joshua chapter four, be sure to use these Spiritual Markers as opportunities to share God's love and activity on your family's behalf with your children and grandchildren.

> › **Note:** In 1 Samuel 7:12, Samuel named the stone "Ebenezer" which means "stone of help."

Spiritual Markers Journaling—Timeline Method

A Spiritual Marker identifies a time of decision, direction, or transition when you clearly knew that God guided you.

In Scripture we see at each new step in His divine plan, God involved a person. Often in the call, God rehearsed His previous activity so the individual could see God's perspective on what was happening at that moment.

When God gets ready for you to take a new step or direction in His activity, it will always be in sequence with what He has already been doing in your life. Every act of God builds on the past with a view toward the future.

God was accomplishing His purposes for your life prior to your birth, and He has been active in your life since you were born (see Jeremiah 1:5). When God is ready for you to take a new step or direction in His activity, it will always be in sequence with what He has already been doing in your life. God builds your character in an orderly fashion with a divine purpose in mind.

Materials:

- Blank journal or composition book
- Pen or pencil

Method:

Step 1: Sit quietly with the Lord.

Step 2: Think over your life and list the major events as they come to mind. If it is easier, you might divide the length of your lifetime into shorter time periods. (For example, a person who is sixty years old might divide that time period into three twenty-year periods or six ten-year periods.)

Step 3: Over the next hours, or even days, continue to add major life events to your timeline as you think of them.

Step 4: Create your timeline by putting the major life events into chronological order.

Step 5: Using your timeline, pull out your Spiritual Markers.

Step 6: Review your timeline and your Spiritual Markers from time to time.

> › Use your Spiritual Markers as reminders of God's awesome power and His mighty acts on your behalf.

> › Allow this insight to give you confidence to meet new challenges and to see how God has been growing you.

> › Like the memorial stones of Joshua in chapter four, be sure to use these Spiritual Markers as opportunities to share God's love and activity on your family's behalf with your children and grandchildren.

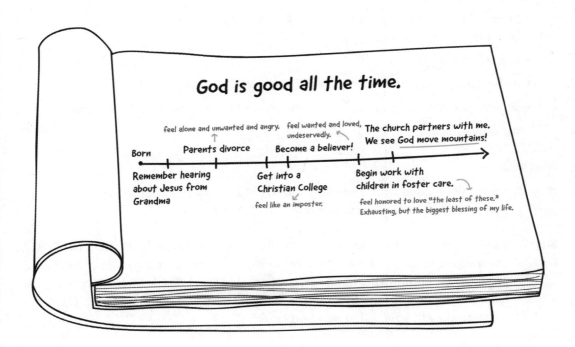

Vision Board/Vision Map Journaling

A Vision Board (also called a Vision Map) is a tool used to help clarify, concentrate, and maintain focus on a specific life goal. For a Christian, this board can be a reflection of your personal mission statement, or it can help keep you focused on growing in Christlikeness.

There has been huge debate over whether Christians should engage in creating vision boards. As with so many other things (prayer, fasting, meditation—to name a few), we must keep our eyes on Christ and on our heart so that this process does not become perverted.

Spend time alone with God as you plan and make preparation for your vision board. Spend time with Him in prayer as you go through the process, and again at points afterward as you use your board for periods of self-reflection.

Materials:

- Sheet of poster board, large cardstock, blank journal page, or photo editing program
- Scripture passages
- Inspiring quotes
- Words, phrases, images cut from magazines or printed from the computer
- Adhesive

Method:

Step 1: Spend time alone with God. Ask Him to help you define your vision. Ask Him for a passion if you do not yet have one.

Step 2: As you select Scripture for your Vision Board, go to the Bible. Read it. Don't just use a verse because it seems to fit or because others are using it. Read the entire verse. Read around the verse. Discover the context. Look at cross references. Seek the meaning of the Scripture. Ask for wisdom and understanding. Does the passage truly fit your vision and purpose?

Step 3: Create your board using Scripture, inspiring quotes, words, and images you have collected. Items can simply be written and drawn onto a poster board or other paper. Alternately, they can be cut from magazines or other sources and glued on or produced using word processing and/or photo editing programs.

Step 4: Spend more time alone with God as you go through the process of creating your Vision Board.

Step 5: Use your completed Vision Board for scheduled times of self-reflection. For example: If your Vision Board represents your five-year vision, schedule yearly or every-six-month checks.

Step 6: Use your completed Vision Board as you commune with God.

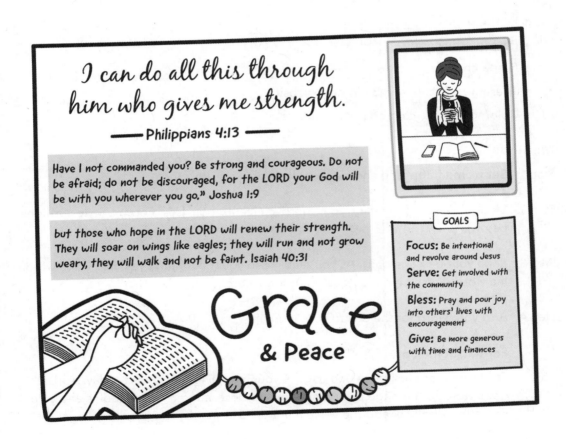

Word-a-Day Journaling

This method of journaling is for the lover of words or anyone who wants to go deeper by paying attention to words.

Word-a-Day is a Scripture journaling method that asks its participants to concentrate on a single passage of Scripture for a period of several days (Lent, Advent, a particular month, or any specified time). Each day during the designated time period, the Word-a-Day journaler then zeroes in on a different word from the passage.

Materials:

- Blank journal or composition book
- Pen or pencil
- Passage of Scripture
- Research tools:
- Thesaurus, Dictionary, Bible-help website
- Colored pencils, colored pens, markers

Method:

Step 1: Set a time frame and choose a passage of Scripture.

Step 2: Decide on the format of your word concentration (see Format/Style Options below).

Step 3: Read your passage daily. As you read, keep your heart and eyes open for a word. If a word doesn't jump out, ask God for a word.

Step 4: Add your word for the day to your journal.

Format/Style Options:

Study in Color. Designate one page in your journal for your word-a-day. Add each day's word to the page by writing it in and decorating it with doodles and color. For later reference, add the verse number to or nearby the word.

Word Study. Set up one page in your journal for each word. Write your word across the top of the page and include the verse number. Dig deeper into the word by looking up and recording its definition, synonyms, cross-references, and any other information you choose.

Soul Friendship
Journaling

Soul Friendship *is the spiritual practice of engaging fellow disciples of Jesus in prayerful conversation or other spiritual practices. It is an intimate, life-giving relationship that helps you pay attention to the activity of God in your life and that helps you respond to His activity.*

Cheer Notes Journaling

Journaling is a tool for soul care, and one way we care for our souls is through soul friendships.

Several times in the New Testament we are commanded to encourage one another and to build one another up (see 1 Thessalonians 4:8, 5:11; Hebrews 3:13, 10:24–25).

Invest in your soul friendships through journaling. Encourage, build up, and love your friends with Cheer Notes.

Materials:

- Cardstock, blank cards, or other appropriate paper
- Bible: verses of Scripture
- Pens, pencils, colored pens, colored pencils, markers
- Stamps and stamp pads
- Stickers
- Paint
- Other assorted art supplies

Method:

Step 1: Select a meaningful verse of Scripture. Write the Scripture on your Cheer Note.

In addition to the Scripture verse (or in place of the Scripture verse), you may want to write out your thoughts on the Scripture, what God has been teaching you about it, a quote or song lyrics relating to the Scripture, or anything else you choose.

Step 2: Decorate and embellish your note.

Step 3: Mail it or hand deliver it to your friend as a means of encouragement, love, and building up.

Soul Searching
Journaling

Soul Searching, *or personal reflection, is the spiritual practice of paying attention in order that we might grow in our love for God and others. Soul searching is very important to the health of the soul. This practice helps to reveal the things that draw us away from God.*

A Journaling Check-Up for Your Soul

In her book, *Discovering Soul Care*, Mindy Caliguire explains that even though our soul's voice is difficult to hear, we can and must learn to hear it.[9]

Searching the soul is not an easy task. It is, in fact, a very difficult and humbling experience. But as hard as it is, the benefits are worth it. For it is through the recognizing, acknowledging, and releasing to God of the very hard personal things in our lives that we are drawn closer to Him.

Materials:

- Blank journal or composition book
- Pen or pencil

Method:

Step 1: In your journal, brainstorm a list of words to describe the current condition of your soul. Use the words to the right to get started. Include any words that come to mind.

Step 2: Next, set up a two-column list in your journal. Head the columns "Neglected" and "Healthy." Then place each of your words from Step 1 into the appropriate column.

Step 3: Reflect on your two-columned list.

› Is your soul healthy or is it showing major signs of neglect?

› How do you feel about your assessment? Are you resisting what appears on your list? Are you embracing it? Accepting it? Does it feel false? Hopeless? Desirable?

Step 4: Write your thoughts and reflections from Step 3 in your journal.

Step 5: Take the results of your self-assessment to God in prayer. Ask Him to reveal your areas of greatest need and to help you nourish your soul back to health.

9. Mindy Caliguire, *Discovering Soul Care* (Downers Grove: InterVarsity Press, 2007), 14–19.

Daily Dot Points Journaling

Recording Daily Dot Points is a quick way to create a record of what is currently going on in your life.

Additionally, the entries, whether singly or collectively, become an effective tool for *self-reflection:*

Reflect upon current entries in order to gain clarity and understanding into your circumstances or to discover what God is teaching you.

Reflect upon Daily Dot Points one year, five years, or ten years later in order to see spiritual growth.

Materials:

- Blank journal or composition book
- Pen or pencil

Method:

Step 1: Record the date, your location, and your mood at the top of your page.

Step 2: Write down just a couple of Daily Dot Points about what is going on in your life. Generally speaking, Daily Dot Points are circumstances or events.

Step 3: Add more to the dot points when you feel the need. This should be a once-in-a-while addition, however. The idea behind Daily Dot Points is to keep it short and simple.

Step 4: Daily Dot Points are not limited to circumstances and events. Sometimes your dot points might be things that are bothering you or questions that are rolling around in your mind.

Fears Journaling

Give all your worries and cares to God, for he cares about you (1 Peter 5:7, NLT).

"Give all your worries and cares…" Our fears do not disappoint our God. He knows we have them.

The issue is not that we have fears, it's how we handle them. Satan is cunning. He would like nothing more than to immobilize us with our fears. Don't allow yourself to be immobilized. Take your fears to God through journaling.

Materials:

- Blank journal or composition book
- Pen or pencil

Method:

Step 1: *Begin with prayer.* Ask God to give you the courage to write about your fears openly.

Step 2: *Write.* There is no one way to Fears Journal. Choose one of the following, combine one or two, or develop a method of your own.

Just write—freely, as the thoughts come.

List your fears. Include how they are playing out in your life if you desire.

Identify your fear(s) and consider the source. Then search the Bible for verses and passages that refute the fears.

Single out a fear. Then write a good-bye letter to it.

Step 3: *Pray again.* God loves you more than you can know. He can be trusted *with* your fears and *in* your fears. Instead of keeping your fears all locked up and being immobilized by them, pour them out to Him. Take your fears to Him as you pray about what you have written.

"Self-Counsel" Journaling

It is a fact: we talk to ourselves. According to research, we speak to our souls somewhere between 47,000 and 51,000 sentences a day. Some of this self-talk is neutral, as in, "Where did I put my keys?" and "Don't forget to pick up the kids from ball practice." Much of it is unhealthy, however, such as, "There's no way I can do this. Why does this ALWAYS happen to me?"

Huge problems arise from the fact that we settle into a habit of listening to our self-talk. When we do this, we allow our thoughts to affect our attitude which then leads to a wedge in our relationship with God. This then gets reflected into our earthy relationships.

In *Write Changes: Stories of Transformation Through Journal Writing*, Kim Young explains that Self-Counsel Journaling is a method for learning to recognize destructive self-talk, invoking an immediate STOP, and speaking the truth of the gospel to ourselves with intentionality.[10]

Materials:

- Blank journal or composition book
- Pen or pencil
- Bible (physical or online version)

Method:

Step 1: *Be Aware.* Pay attention to the conversation taking place in your mind. Learn to recognize when your self-talk is unhealthy (full of lies).

Step 2: *Stop.* Put an end to the conversation as soon as you recognize it. Do not allow it to go on another second.

Step 3: *Take ownership of your struggles.* Write your struggles in your journal. Record your conversation, share your thoughts and emotions around the issue, name the lie/sin at the root of the struggle.

10. Kim Young, "Journaling as 'Self-Counsel,'" *Write Changes: Stories of Transformation through Journal Writing* (Sneads Ferry, NC: Write Changes Publishing, 2017), 4–10.

Step 4: *Refocus.* Turn your focus from yourself, toward the truth of the gospel. Search the Scriptures for verses and passages that counter the identified lie(s) with biblical truth. Write them out and meditate on them. Or refocus your mind by journaling through Colossians chapter three. Meditate on these Scripture passages immediately and throughout your day. If you choose, write out a prayer to God as part of your self-counsel journaling entry.

Step 5: *Practice.* Prepare a battle plan for combating future negative self-talk and struggles centered on these same lies. Right there on your journal page, write out very specific and practical ways that will help you stop, refocus, and live the truth of the gospel.

Self-Reflection through Questions Journaling

Soul searching is very important to the health of the soul, but it is not an easy task. In fact, it can be a very difficult and humbling experience, one that at times can even be extremely painful.

Through self-reflection we learn more about ourselves than we ever knew before—hard things that need to be acknowledged and dealt with.

The practice is hard, but so beneficial. It is through recognizing, acknowledging, and releasing to God the very hard things that we are drawn closer to Him.

Materials:

- Blank journal or composition book
- Pen or pencil
- List of questions (located on the following page)

Method:

Step 1: Plan ahead for this time by putting it on your calendar, locating a quiet place as free from distractions as possible, and having your needed materials.

Step 2: Date your journal entry. You might even want to record the time of day, your location, and your mood.

Step 3: Look over the list of questions on the following page. Decide whether you will answer each one, the ones that "jump" out at you, or a certain number of them. While answering all of them in one sitting would be overwhelming to most, unless they had designated an entire day or weekend to the task, setting up a regular system of answering a certain number (such as three or five) each time might be more manageable.

Step 4: As you read through the questions, commit to answering them honestly even if the truth is hard. Take some time. Do not hurry this task.

Questions for Self-Reflection Journaling

- Am I hearing from God?

- Have I lost my joy?

- Am I producing spiritual fruit?

- Am I experiencing victory in my life?

- Have I grown in the last five years? In the last year?

- Do I love God more today than I did before?

- How well am I obeying His Word?

- What are the priorities in my life?

- In what areas of my life am I still not putting God first?

- What in my past is interfering with me doing God's will?

- Do I always try to have an "attitude of gratitude," or do I find myself often complaining about my circumstances?

- In what areas of my life am I ungrateful?

- Have I gotten angry and easily blown up at people?

- Have I been sarcastic?

- What in my past is still causing me fear or anxiety?

- In what past dealing was I dishonest?

- Have I exaggerated myself to make me look better?

- In what areas of my past have I practiced false humility?

- Have I pretended to live one way in front of my Christian friends and another way at home or at work?

- Am I investing my life into the lives of others?

Spiritual Growth Journaling

For this very reason, make every effort to supplement your faith with virtue, and virtue with knowledge, and knowledge with self-control, and self-control with steadfastness, and steadfastness with godliness, and godliness with brotherly affection, and brotherly affection with love. For if these qualities are yours and are increasing, they keep you from being ineffective or unfruitful in the knowledge of our Lord Jesus Christ. For whoever lacks these qualities is so nearsighted that he is blind, having forgotten that he was cleansed from his former sins (2 Peter 1:5–9, ESV).

We are instructed to "make every effort" toward spiritual growth. This growth can be experienced through many means including Scripture study and prayer. Another way we can make an effort to grow is through the discipline of journaling.

Materials:

- Blank journal or composition book
- Pen or pencil
- Optional: list of journaling prompts (located on the following page)

Method:

Step 1: Choose a journaling prompt. Prompts can be found on the following page, at dedicated websites such as Journaling4Faith or the National Association for Christian Journal Writers, or via a Pinterest or Google search.

Step 2: Copy your chosen prompt into your journal.

Step 3: Directly below the prompt, write whatever comes to your mind in response to it (thoughts, reflections, questions, etc.).

Step 4: Date your entry.

Spiritual Growth Journaling Prompts

- My favorite passage of Scripture is… because…
- One lesson I learned from God's Word this week is…
- Three ways I want God to transform me are…
- Two ways I can apply the gospel to my life are…
- An aspect of God's character He recently revealed to me is…
- I find I connect best with God when I…
- I find I feel God's presence most when…
- I hear God saying…
- God has equipped me…
- This week I am struggling with…
- I am waiting for…
- I am anxious about…
- Recently, I found myself wearing the mask of…
- Right now, I see myself as…
- Thank you, Lord, for the blessing of…
- I feel content when…
- Contentment is…
- What brings me the most joy in life is…
- My spiritual gifts/talents/characteristics are…
- I'm encouraged today by…
- God is growing me in…
- A look at how I spent this past day/week reveals…
- An area of my spiritual life where I need to seek the Holy Spirit's guidance is…
- I sit at the feet of Jesus…
- The truth is…
- The area where I need to put more trust in God is…
- My relationship with God…
- Jesus, You are Lord of…
- I'm eager for God to…
- Have I grown in the last month/year? How?

Truth Journaling

In 2 Corinthians 10:5 (ESV), we are commanded to *take every thought captive*. A couple of years ago, the Lord began to speak to me about the difference between listening to myself (continually listening to the onslaught of inner dialogue that occurs in my mind daily) and talking to myself (making a hard stop to the listening and, rather, intentionally speaking truth to myself). Since becoming acquainted with it, I have consciously tried to observe this practice.

Imagine my excitement as a journaler when I came across this renewing of the mind technique in journaling form! In her book, *The Renewing of the Mind Project*, Barb Raveling discusses the idea of Truth Journaling by taking readers through this same process on paper.[11] Just like the thinking-it-in-my-head method, Truth Journaling is an act of intention aimed at taking thoughts captive, examining them, and discerning truth. The added benefit of journaling the process, however, is that this method adds a physical dimension to the process.

Materials:

- Journal or composition book
- Pen or pencil
- Bible or online Bible site

Method:

Step 1: Write out your thoughts. Don't take time to think, just spill them out in all their mess. You may even recognize an untruth as you write. Just keep writing. This part will not be pretty and will generally turn out to be an unorganized mess. There are no time or writing limits, but this step will usually take one to two minutes and produce six to seven sentences.

Step 2: Go back and number each sentence or thought. As gut-level writing, your entry may contain compound or run-on sentences. Be sure you are numbering each separate thought. This will force you to look at each thought running rampant in your head rather than at the whole overwhelming situation.

Step 3: Once numbered, look at each sentence or thought one at a time. Determine whether it is truth or a lie.

Step 4: If it is truth, write "truth." If the statement is a lie, rewrite it so that it is completely true. Your truth statements can be written below your original entry. Be sure to include the corresponding number from step two.

11. Barb Raveling, "Truth Journaling," in "Renew Your Mind," *BarbRaveling* (blog), May 24, 2018, https://barbraveling.com/2012/03/20/rom-tool-1-truth-journaling/. Raveling is also the author of *The Renewing of the Mind Project: Going to God for Help with Your Habits, Goals, and Emotions*, Truthway Press, 2015, and *Taste for Truth: A 30 Day Weight Loss Bible Study*, Truthway Press, 2013.

Truth Journaling: The List Method

Barb Raveling developed another method for Truth Journaling. This method is called "The List Method."[12]

In this form of journaling, writers begin by asking a question of themselves (see step 1). They proceed to list as many answers (beliefs) as they are able. Finally, they go through those beliefs one by one to discern and record the truth.

Materials:

- Journal or composition book
- Pen or pencil
- Bible or online Bible site

Method:

Step 1: Ask yourself a question:

> - What am I believing that is causing me not to want to work on my goal?
> - What am I assuming that is making me want to continue my bad habit?
> - What am I believing about myself, this person, or this situation?
> - List as many responses as you can come up with.

Step 2: Go through the list of responses one by one. Determine whether each is a truth or a lie.

Step 3: If the statement is truth, write "truth." If the statement is a lie, record the truth.

Example:

I'm trying to develop the habit of daily exercise, but I am struggling. After a few days without exercise I decide to truth journal with the list method. I begin by asking myself, "What am I believing about exercise that causes me not to want to do it?"

My list:

- I don't enjoy it.
- I don't have time.
- It doesn't make that much difference.

The Truth:

- Some things are not enjoyable but still need to be done, like dusting.
- I make time for the things I want to do.
- I may not notice it, but exercise is proven to be beneficial to both my health and well-being.

12. Raveling, "Truth Journaling: The List Method," in "Renew Your Mind," *BarbRaveling* (blog), May 24, 2018, https://barbraveling.com/2012/03/27/truth-journaling-the-list-method/.

Journaling
Challenges

ABCDEFGHIJKLMNOPQRSTUVWXYZ
abcdefghijklmnopqrstuvwxyz

ABCDEFGHIJKLMNOPQRSTUVWXYZ
abcdefghijklmnopqrstuvwxyz

ABCDEFGHIJKLMNOPQRSTUVWXYZ

ABCDEFGHIJKLMNOPQRSTUVWXYZ

ABCDEFGHIJKLMNOPQRSTUVWXYZ

ABCDEFGHIJKLMNOPQRSTUVWXYZ

ABCDEFGHIJKLMNOPQRSTUVWXYZ

ABCDEFGHIJKLMNOPQRSTUVWXYZ
abcdefghijklmnopqrstuvwxyz

Journaling Challenges

- Journal your Sunday school lessons.

- Journal your small group material.

- Journal your sermon notes.

- Journal your identity "In Christ." *

- Journal Scriptures of Praise. *

- Journal the names of Christ. *

- Journal the attributes of God. *

- Journal the "I Wills" of the book of Psalms.

- Journal through the words of Jesus.

- Journal through the miracles of Jesus.

- Journal through the promises of God.

- Journal through the parables of Jesus.

- Journal through the lineage of Jesus (Jesse Tree Journaling). *

- Journal through the women of the Bible.

- Journal the "tongue" (verses regarding our speech).

- Journal through "love" (verses on love).

- Journal through "anger" (verses on anger).

- Journal through "joy" (verses on joy).

- Journal your favorite praise songs/hymns, with corresponding Scripture.

- Journal through Psalm 119.

- Journal through one entire book of the Bible.

- Journal one entry for each book of the Bible.

* Reference sheets are included on the following pages.

Attributes of God for Journaling *

- Eternality—God never runs out of resources. (Psalm 90:2)

- Faithfulness—God can be trusted to provide for me. (2 Timothy 2:13)

- Goodness—God generously gives to me. (Psalm 86:5)

- Grace—God is compassionate toward me. (Ephesians 2:4)

- Holiness—God provides guidelines for pure living. (Leviticus 19, Isaiah 6:3)

- Immutability—God never changes His action toward me. (James 1:17)

- Jealousy—God is "fanatical" in His protection of me. (Exodus 34:14)

- Love—God has made me His child. (1 John 3:1)

- Omnipotence—God is strong enough to care for me. (Jeremiah 32:17)

- Omniscience—God knows all I need to live successfully. (Psalm 139:1)

- Patience—God waits for me to change to be like Him. (2 Peter 3:9)

- Presence—God is always with me. (Hebrews 13:5)

- Righteousness—God will do what is right concerning me. (Romans 2:6)

- Self-Sufficiency—God is not dependent on others for my life. (Exodus 3:14)

- Sovereignty—God graciously directs every event of life. (Ephesians 1:11)

- Truth—God has absolute standards for me. (Numbers 23:19)

- Wisdom—God gives me wisdom to live successfully. (1 Corinthians 1:20-26)

* A partial list.

The Lineage of Jesus (Jesse Tree) for Journaling *

Abraham	Jotham
Isaac	Ahaz
Jacob	Hezekiah
Judah	Manasseh
Perez	Amos
Hezron	Josiah
Ram	Jechoniah
Amminadab	Shealtiel
Nahshon	Zerubbabel
Salmon	Abiud
Boaz (by Rahab)	Eliakim
Obed (by Ruth)	Azor
Jesse	Zadok
David	Achim
Solomon	Eliud
Rehoboam	Eleazar
Abijah	Matthan
Asaph	Jacob
Jehoshaphat	Joseph (the husband of Mary)
Joram	Jesus
Uzziah	

* From Matthew 1.

My Identity In Christ Scriptures for Journaling *

Genesis 1:27

Deuteronomy 31:8

Psalm 18:35

Psalm 139:13–16

Proverbs 8:35

Isaiah 1:18

Isaiah 62:5

Jeremiah 29:11

Jeremiah 31:3

Zephaniah 3:17

John 15:15

Romans 6:23

Romans 8:1

Romans 8:15

Romans 8:17

Romans 8:32

Romans 8:37

Romans 12:2

1 Corinthians 1:2

1 Corinthians 3:9

1 Corinthians 6:11

1 Corinthians 6:17

1 Corinthians 6:19

2 Corinthians 2:15

2 Corinthians 3:12

2 Corinthians 5:17

2 Corinthians 5:20

2 Corinthians 5:21

2 Corinthians 6:14

Galatians 2:20

Galatians 3:13

Galatians 3:26

Galatians 5:1

Ephesians 1:4

Ephesians 1:5

Ephesians 1:13

Ephesians 2:5

Ephesians 2:6

Ephesians 2:10

Philippians 4:7

Colossians 1:13

Colossians 2:10

2 Thessalonians 2:13

1 Timothy 1:9

Titus 2:14

1 John 3:1

1 John 4:10

1 John 5:5

1 Peter 2:9

1 Peter 2:24

* A partial list.

Scriptures of Praise for Journaling *

Exodus 15:11—There is None Like God

Exodus 15:26—The Lord Who Heals

Exodus 34:6–7—He is Slow to Anger

Deuteronomy 7:9—A Faithful God

Nehemiah 9:6—God the Creator

Nehemiah 9:17—A Forgiving God

Nehemiah 9:31—A Merciful God

Psalm 3:3—The Lifter of My Head

Psalm 18:2—My Rock, My Fortress,
My Deliverer

Psalm 18:30—His Way is Perfect

Psalm 21:6—God of Joy

Psalm 23:1–3—The Lord My Shepherd

Psalm 27:1—My Light and My Salvation

Psalm 30:11—The One Who Turns it All Around

Psalm 62:7—My Refuge

Psalm 68:19—The One Who Daily Bears
My Burdens

Psalm 70:5—My Liberator

Psalm 77:14—The God of Miracles

Psalm 89:8—The Almighty God

Psalm 116:8–9—The Deliverer of My
Entire Being

Isaiah 9:6—The Everlasting Father

Isaiah 40:28—His Understanding is
Unsearchable

Isaiah 45:5—The Only God

Isaiah 54:5—The God of All the Earth

Isaiah 65:24—The God Who Answers Prayer

Jeremiah 32:17—Nothing is Too Difficult
for Him

Lamentations 3:23—A Faithful God

Daniel 7:9—The Ancient of Days

Matthew 8:11—A Personal God

Mark 8:2—The One Who Responds to My
Weak Flesh with Compassion

Luke 4:18—The Restorer of My Sight

John 1:16—The One Who Gives to Me from
His Fullness

John 3:16—A Giving God

Romans 3:26—A God of Justice

Romans 16:20—The Lord Our Peace

2 Corinthians 1:3—The God of All Comfort

2 Corinthians 2:14—The One Who Triumphs

2 Corinthians 9:8—God Who Provides

1 Timothy 6:15—King of Kings and Lord
of Lords

Hebrews 13:8—The Same Yesterday,
Today, Forever

2 Peter 3:9—A Patient, Persevering God

1 John 3:16—He Laid Down His Life for Me

1 John 4:7–8—God is Love

1 John 4:16—A Loving God

Jude 25—Eternal, Saving God

Revelation 4:8—The Holy One

* A partial list.

The Names of Christ for Journaling *

A Chief Cornerstone (1 Peter 2:6)

Chief Shepherd (1 Peter 5:4)

Christ Jesus (1 Timothy 1:15)

Christ the Lord (Luke 2:11)

I AM (John 8:58)

Jesus (Matthew 1:21)

King of Israel (John 12:13)

Lamb of God (John 1:29)

Living Water (John 4:10)

Lord Jesus (Acts 7:59)

Lord of All (Acts 10:36)

My Savior (2 Peter 3:18)

Ruler of the Kings of the Earth
(Revelation 1:5)

Son (John 3:17; 1 John 4:14)

Son of God (John 1:34; Matthew 16:16)

Son of Man (John 1:51; John 12:23)

The Advocate (1 John 2:1)

The Bread of Life (John 6:35)

The Day Star (2 Peter 1:19)

The Faithful Witness (Revelation 1:5)

The Firstborn from the Dead
(Revelation 1:5)

The Foundation (1 Corinthians 3:11)

The Gift of God (John 4:10)

The Good Shepherd (John 10:11)

The Holy One of God (Mark 1:24)

The Life (John 14:6)

The Light (John 3:19; John 12:35)

The Light of the World (John 9:5)

The One and Only (John 1:14)

The Only Begotten Son of God (John 3:18)

The Prince of Peace (Isaiah 9:6)

The Resurrection and the Life (John 11:25)

The Rock (Matthew 16:18)

The Root of Jesse (Isaiah 11:10)

The Temple (John 2:9; Revelation 21:22)

The True Light (John 1:9)

The True Vine (John 15:1)

The Truth (John 14:6)

The Way (John 14:6)

The Word (John 1:1)

* A partial list.

Brief Overview of Some Additional Journaling Methods

This collection of journaling methods is certainly not limited in its use. Locate one or more that fit your style and personality. Then use it/them to journal your prayers, Scripture, gratitude, your Spiritual journey, or any other topic.

Bullet Journaling

Bullet Journaling is a note-taking system created by Ryder Carroll, a digital product designer located in Brooklyn, New York.[13]

To Bullet Journal for the care of your soul, choose whether you will use your journal for one specific task (prayer, for example) or across several disciplines (prayer, Scripture, gratitude). If using it for the purpose of collecting information across two or more disciplines, divide your journal into major sections and label each section. If using it for only one discipline, decide if you would like to divide your notebook into smaller labeled sections (prayer requests, answers to prayer, Scriptures about prayer, my recorded prayers).

Once your journal is set up, begin collecting information—bullet style.

Cluster Journaling

Clustering is often referred to as brainstorming, brain dumping, or mind mapping. This journaling technique works well when ideas just don't seem to flow on their own. It also works well when there are so many thoughts and ideas in your head, you don't know where to start in writing them coherently on a page.

To cluster, write your overarching topic (see examples on the next page) in the center of your page and circle it. Then, without stopping to think, begin to write. As they come to mind, add words to your page, placing them in new bubbles. Make associations as the page develops. Tie ideas to each other and to the main idea by drawing lines to connect them. Your completed journal page will be a complex matrix of ideas, many of which you didn't even know you had.

Later, if you choose, use your completed Cluster Journaling page to write a cohesive piece that more accurately conveys your thoughts.

---

13. Ryder Carroll, "Bullet Journal," http://bulletjournal.com/.

Examples:

You keep running into the same word or concept (Sabbath rest, stillness, grace). Write that word or concept in the center of your page. Then add your recollections, thoughts, and ideas regarding that topic as the next step.

You are looking for a different way to engage in praise and worship of God. Choose a name for God that is particularly precious to you and place it in the center of your page. Create your cluster by recording His attributes as they come to your mind.

Conversation Journaling

Conversations are an excellent way to gain insight. Write your journal entry in the form of a dialogue and talk with anyone (or anything)! Converse with one or more of the Bible characters in your passage of study, talk with the subject of a Christian biography you are reading, write out a conversation with God, or even record a dialogue you are having with yourself.

List Journaling

This is simple. Lists are quick and easy and can be made from anything. Make a list of your sermon notes, prayer requests, things you are thankful for, recurring words in a Scripture passage, the attributes of God, words and ideas related to something God is teaching you, or the main points of a chapter of Scripture. The ideas for List Journaling are nearly endless.

Prompt Journaling

Journal prompts are targeted and get your thoughts to flow. Provided in many forms—words, phrases, statements, questions, and images—prompts help your mind make the shift from thinking about what to write to answering a question or completing a thought. Prompts can be useful in any journaling for the soul area (prayer, Scripture engagement, self-reflection, gratitude).

Scrapbook Journaling (Faithbooking)

Scrapbook Journaling is a creative expression of your time spent with God. In a scrapbook, art journal, or even a composition book, combine Scripture, thoughts, quotes, prayers, photographs, stories, fancy paper, and other embellishments to record what you are learning and how you are growing. Scrapbook Journaling works well with almost all of the spiritual disciplines (prayer, Scripture study, self-reflection, gratitude, and spiritual journey).

Timed Journaling

Timed Journaling is just that—timed! It is a process that encourages quick entries filled with thought. Simply set the timer on your phone (or any other timer) and write. Keep your pen or pencil moving the entire time and be sure to stop immediately when the timer goes off.

Journaling Templates

These templates are designed to jump start your journaling process. Purchase some lightweight, transparent paper such as tracing paper, parchment, or carbon paper, at your local craft store.

Lay the paper over (or under, depending on the type of paper you have purchased) the template, and trace onto your new paper. Then you can use your traced sheet to color or decorate any way you want.

Great is his faithfulness;
HIS MERCIES BEGIN AFRESH
EACH MORNING.
LAMENTATIONS 3:23 (NLT)

The
peace of God,
WHICH TRANSCENDS ALL UNDERSTANDING,
WILL guard YOUR
hearts
& your
minds
in Christ Jesus.
Philippians 4:7 (NIV)

I will lie down AND SLEEP IN PEACE. O LORD, You alone keep me safe.

PSALM 4:8 (NLV)

YOU ARE IN Christ Jesus, WHO HAS BECOME... our RIGHTEOUSNESS, HOLINESS, & redemption.

1 COR 1:30 (NIV)

AS PART OF

God's sovereign plan

WE WERE

chosen

FROM THE BEGINNING

to be his. *EPHESIANS 1:1 (TLB)*

YOU WILL KEEP HIM

in perfect peace,

WHOSE MIND IS STAYED ON YOU,

BECAUSE HE TRUSTS IN YOU.

ISAIAH 26:3 (NKJV)

Other Resources by Deborah Haddix

- *Praying with Purpose: Taking Your Prayer Life from Vague to Victorious*—Prayer is the most precious gift we can give our family, friends and loved ones, and this book offers a roadmap for enjoying and sharing a focused and creative prayer life. For those who often pray vague prayers, this book has many suggestions and resources compiled to encourage and inspire victorious praying.

- Digging Deeper KIDS (3 Options)
    - › Digging Deeper KIDS Methods includes 9 different techniques for helping children engage with the Word of God.
    - › Kids' Journaling Templates are perfect for the child who is intimidated by a blank page or as "training wheels" for the Digging Deeper Kids Methods.
    - › The Digging Deeper Kids BUNDLE includes both The Digging Deeper Methods AND The Digging Deeper Journaling Templates.

- *Soul Nourishment: Satisfying Our Deep Longing for God*—a gentle reminder of the importance of soul care. It is also a handbook for today's busy woman—filled with a multitude of easy, ready-to-use resources intended to aid in nourishing the soul.

- Scripture Journaling Workbook—A basic "how-to" of Scripture journaling. Includes creative lettering tips and practice in creative doodling and lettering.

- *Digging Deeper: Journaling Templates for Adults*—Journaling templates are perfect for the person who prefers "filling in" the blanks or anyone who may be intimidated by a blank page. This set comes as a PDF download and includes 17 Journaling templates.

For more information on these and other resources by Deborah Haddix, visit deborah-haddix.com

Bibliography

Batterson, Mark. *Draw the Circle: The 40 Day Prayer Challenge*. Grand Rapids: Zondervan, 2012.

Caliguire, Mindy. *Discovering Soul Care*. Downers Grove, IL: InterVarsity Press, 2007.

Carroll, Ryder. *Bullet Journal*. http://bulletjournal.com.

de Cruz, Betsy. "When You Want More out of Time with God." *Faith Spilling Over* (blog). May 24, 2018. http://faithspillingover.com/2015/07/07/when-you-want-more-out-of-time-with-god/#more-2401.

Hillegass, Clifton Keith. *CliffsNotes*. New York: Houghton Mifflin Harcourt, 2012.

K & Company, LLC. Smash Journals.: Sold on numerous crafting websites.

MacBeth, Sybil. *Praying in Color: Drawing a New Path to God*. Brewster, MA: Paraclete Press, 2013.

Merriam-Webster.com, s.v. "Gratitude," accessed May 31, 2018, https://www.merriam-webster.com/dictionary/gratitude.

Merriam-Webster.com, s.v. "Inductive," accessed May 30, 2018, https://www.merriam-webster.com/dictionary/inductive.

Raveling, Barb. "Truth Journaling." In "Renew Your Mind." *BarbRaveling* (blog). May 24, 2018. https://barbraveling.com/2012/03/20/rom-tool-1-truth-journaling/.

———. "Truth Journaling: The List Method." In "Renew Your Mind." *BarbRaveling* (blog). May 24, 2018. https://barbraveling.com/2012/03/27/truth-journaling-the-list-method/.

Wynalda, Rob. *Journible: The 17:18 Series*. Grand Rapids: Reformation Heritage Books, 2009—2015.

Young, Kim. "Journaling as 'Self-Counsel.'" In *Write Changes: Stories of Transformation Through Journal Writing*. Sneads Ferry, NC: Write Changes Publishing, 2017.

Practice Pages

Practice Pages

Practice Pages

Practice Pages

Practice Pages